Praise for *Encouraging the Heart*

"Jim and Barry's book is a powerful reminder of the importance of heart, love, and courage in the workplace. Their ideas on improving the work experience and the relationship between manager and employee are accessible to everyone, regardless of their educational background. The authors have consistently emphasized these values in organizations worldwide, using compelling examples and stories of everyday leaders to illustrate their points. They remind us that we are all in this together, especially as the world changes and competition intensifies. This book is a must-read for anyone looking to enhance retention, engagement, and development in their organization. If you ever need a reminder of these essential principles, just turn to any chapter for inspiration."

—Dr. Beverly Kaye
Co-author of *Love 'Em or Lose 'Em: Getting Good People to Stay,*
Help Them Grow or Watch Them Go, and
Up Is Not the Only Way: Rethinking Career Mobility

"When I first read *Encouraging the Heart* 20 years ago, it was a revelation. Here were respected leadership gurus Kouzes and Posner talking about so-called 'soft skills' in a way that showed them as a business necessity. For years, I would spot the book on executives' shelves in my travels. It became a standard for leaders who 'got it,' those who grasped that success didn't come from autocratic, demanding leadership but by lifting people up with courage and encouragement. The authors have now updated this classic for the modern day. The case studies and stories are fresh and fun to read. Most importantly, the second edition of *Encouraging the Heart* provides every leader with a wealth of practical tools to answer the most important of questions: *How do I do it?* In other words: *What are the steps I must take to encourage my people, get the best out of my team members, and help my team achieve greater success*? Bravo!"

—Adrian Gostick
New York Times bestselling author of *Leading with Gratitude*

"*Encouraging the Heart* is a transformative guide that touches the essence of leadership—caring for your people. James Kouzes and Barry Posner beautifully articulate the power of recognition and purpose in inspiring greatness in teams. Their approach is practical, evidence-based, and deeply human. As someone who believes in leading with purpose, I can't emphasize enough how important this message is today. Leadership is not about titles or position—it's about connecting with others on a personal level and nurturing their potential. This book will not only ignite purpose within your organization, but it will also help you build a culture where people feel valued, motivated, and truly appreciated. In these pages, you'll discover that when leaders lead with heart, people will give their very best."

—Garry Ridge
Chairman Emeritus of WD-40 Company, and The Culture Coach

"In a time when fear runs high, the need for encouragement runs higher! Grounded in research but written with heart, this book will equip you to embolden the hearts of others to lead from courage, not fear—to step bravely forward in the moments that matter most. The world will be better for it."

—Dr. Margie Warrell
Leadership speaker and bestselling author of *The Courage Gap*

"Kouzes and Posner are the Lennon and McCartney of leadership. Always relevant, insightful, and enduring. Encouraging the Heart is another reminder from them that leadership is more than balance sheets and pivot tables. Leadership is about being human and they show us how to bring that blessing to the workplace."

—Richard A. Moran
author of Never Say Whatever

"In this book, authors Jim Kouzes and Barry Posner are at their best—challenging the traditional thinking around recognition in the workplace. Through their research and the many stories shared, they shine a light on the dual nature of encouraging the heart, highlighting how it is both tough and tender. It is a practical and inspiring read for leaders at all levels!"

—Andrea Butcher
Founder of AE Consulting, and host of Being [at Work]

"This new edition of *Encouraging the Heart* arrives at a pivotal moment. As the most personal of The Leadership Challenge's Five Practices, it delves deep into what truly drives people to achieve: feeling valued and recognized. Jim and

Barry provide an invaluable toolkit for leaders seeking to uplift and inspire their teams, organizations, families, and communities by acknowledging those who uphold shared values and go above and beyond expectations. In a world that can often seem dark, this book is a call to be the light."

—Lori Armstrong
DNP, RN NEA-BC, CEO and Chief Clinical Officer,
Inspire Nurse Leaders

"The bottom line is this: people thrive in environments where they find meaning, recognition, and purpose. When leaders provide those things, remarkable things happen! Kouzes' and Posner's latest is an exceptional handbook for anyone looking to improve their leadership and the lives of those in their span of care!"

—Bob Chapman
CEO of Barry-Wehmiller, author of *Everybody Matters:
The Extraordinary Power of Caring for Your People Like Family*

"I've been a fan of Kouzes and Posner's work for many, many years and am especially excited about the publication of a new edition of Encouraging the Heart: Igniting Purpose and Providing Meaningful Recognition. Employee recognition is often referred to as the Greatest Management Principle in the World, and Encouraging the Heart provides a blueprint for how every leader can best harness the power of this proven principle to drive desired behavior and performance with their employees. It's a delight to read and even more fun to apply! Thank you, Jim and Barry, for helping to show us the way!"

—Bob Nelson PhD,
President of Nelson Motivation Inc.,
creator of Worldwide Employee Appreciation Day,
and bestselling author of 1,501 Ways to Reward Employees

ENCOURAGING
THE
HEART

JAMES M. | **BARRY Z.**
KOUZES | POSNER

Best-Selling Authors of **The Leadership Challenge**

ENCOURAGING
THE
HEART

IGNITING PURPOSE AND
PROVIDING MEANINGFUL RECOGNITION

SECOND EDITION

Published by John Wiley & Sons, Inc., Hoboken, New Jersey.
Published simultaneously in Canada.

For general information on our other products and services or for technical support, please contact our Customer Care Department within the United States at (800) 762-2974, outside the United States at (317) 572-3993 or fax (317) 572-4002.

Wiley also publishes its books in a variety of electronic formats. Some content that appears in print may not be available in electronic formats. For more information about Wiley products, visit our web site at www.wiley.com.

Library of Congress Cataloging-in-Publication Data is Available:

ISBN: 9781394303908 (Paperback)
ISBN: 9781394303915 (ePub)
ISBN: 9781394303922 (ePDF)

Cover Design: Wiley
Cover Image: © f9photos/Getty Images
Author Photos: Courtesy of the Authors

SKY10100189_031825

We dedicate this book to our community of Certified Masters, Partners, and Publishers who have encouraged our hearts for more than four decades. Thank you all for being a vital participant in our mission to increase the quality and quantity of leaders for the world.

CONTENTS

Contents

INTRODUCTION

COURAGE. ENCOURAGE. Two words, same origin: heart.

To quote a classic Broadway musical refrain, "You've gotta have heart. All you really need is heart. . .Miles 'n miles n' miles of heart."[1]

There's no bravery or boldness without heart. There's no spirit or support without heart. There's no sacrifice or soul without heart. Nothing great ever gets done without heart. You've gotta have heart.

At the heart of leadership is caring. Without caring, leadership has no purpose. Without showing others that you care about them, they won't care about you. Leadership is a relationship. It's personal, and it's interpersonal. In the most basic sense, it requires a connection between leaders and constituents over matters of the heart.

We need heart because the struggle to make extraordinary things happen is arduous. Our research tells us that if we're going to make it to the summit, we *need* someone figuratively, if not literally, standing nearby and shouting, "Come on, you can do it. I know you can do it!"

That's not something we readily admit; we often think we can do it alone. But we all really do need encouragement to do our best. Encouragement boosts performance, strengthens our resolve, and improves our health. Otherwise, why perform in front of an audience? Why not just sing in an empty room, play in an empty arena, or sell only to yourself? We need the applause. We need the enthusiasm and the energy from others. To do our best, we need to feel connected to others and, in turn, they to us. Greatness is never achieved alone.

Encouraging the Heart is about the leadership practice that connects us. It signals and documents that we're in "this" together—whatever the project, program, campaign, neighborhood, congregation, division, or endeavor. Social capital joins financial and intellectual capital as the necessary ingredients for organizational success. In creating social capital, leaders encourage the heart so that people will want to be with and for one another.

When leaders commend individuals for honoring the organization's values or achieving its goals, they foster courage, inspiring them to experience their ability to deliver—even when the pressure is on. When we recognize people for their contributions, we expand their awareness of their value to the organization and their coworkers, imparting a sense of social connectedness that all humans seek. While we may all be connected by being human, leaders make sure we're truly *in touch* with one another.

The world has changed since discovering, understanding, and appreciating the importance for leadership of *Encouraging the Heart* more than four decades ago and writing an earlier edition to enable others to engage more effectively in this vital leadership practice. Yet this essential leadership practice could not be timelier or more needed. Nothing on the horizon suggests, moreover, that its importance will diminish.

The Heart of The Matter

Encouraging the Heart discusses the principles and practices that support the basic human need to be appreciated for who we are and what we do. It's about how leaders can apply certain behaviors, principles, and practices to their daily work. This is not a book about glad-handing, backslapping, gold stars, and payoffs. It's about the importance of linking recognition, rewards, and appreciation to standards of excellence. It's about ensuring people know the significance of what they do, why it matters, and its purpose. It's about understanding why encouragement is essential to sustaining people's commitment to organizations and outcomes. It's about acknowledging that it requires hard work to make extraordinary things happen in organizations. It's about finding ways to enhance your ability in—and comfort with—recognizing and celebrating the achievements of others.

Encouraging the Heart originates in our research on the practices of people when they function at their *best as leaders*. Since our studies began more than four decades ago, we've collected thousands of personal-best leadership case studies and analyzed behavioral leadership data from more than five million respondents from around the globe across various individual, functional, and organizational demographics.[2] We've consistently found that when making extraordinary things happen, leaders:

- ▶ Model the Way
- ▶ Inspire a Shared Vision
- ▶ Challenge the Process
- ▶ Enable Others to Act
- ▶ Encourage the Heart

All of The Five Practices of Exemplary Leadership® are essential. They all contribute to explaining why leaders are successful. Each plays a distinct part, and none alone is sufficient. We wrote a book, *The Leadership Challenge*, about all five practices and their impact on engagement and performance. So why have we written a book about only one practice, Encourage the Heart? There are four reasons.

The first is practicality. Over the last few decades, many books have been published about reward and recognition, but they have mostly focused more on techniques than on the underlying principles. We wanted to offer a set of behaviors, principles, practices, and examples to provide leaders with a repeatable process and essential actions they could apply in their own settings.

The second reason is principle. For too long now, we've heard the human side of business referred to as the "soft" side, and encouraging the heart seems about as soft as you can get. Some of our clients even told us the phrase *encourage the heart* wouldn't work in their organizations or cultures and asked if we could change the practice's name. We never have, and we never will. In this book, we will demonstrate that encouraging the heart is not soft; we will also show how powerful a force it is in achieving high standards and stretch goals. If you're after results, then you'd better start paying attention to encouraging the heart.

Third, our work is evidence-based. We've researched leadership for more than forty years and gathered data from millions of leaders an their constituents about The Five Practices of Exemplary Leadership.[3] When we write about leadership and what leaders should do to make extraordinary things happen, we are not simply making assertions based on opinion. We can support what we say with data. We wanted to ensure that in the most recent years—characterized by many challenges, conflicts, and division— the practice of Encourage the Heart remained valid and impactful. You'll find that data in the chapters of this book.

The final reason we chose to write *Encouraging the Heart* is because we wanted to add our voices to the discussion of soul and spirit in the workplace. Leaders create relationships, and one of these relationships is between individuals and their work. Ultimately, we all work for a purpose, and that common purpose must be served when encouraging individuals and groups. Encouraging the heart only works when there's a good fit between the person, the work, and the organization.

To this final point, it is interesting to note that the word *encouragement* has its root in the Latin word *cor,* which literally means "heart."[4] So does the word *courage*. To have courage means to have heart. To *en*courage—to provide with or give courage—means to give others heart.

Richard I, king of England from 1189 to 1199, was glorified for his courage. What did the troubadours call him? Richard the Lionheart.

The heroic tradition from which this language comes tells us that when discussing courage and encouragement, we don't simply mean the sentimental notion expressed on contemporary greeting cards. Rather, in this context, the word *heart* brings forth images of courage when faced with significant challenges, hope when confronted with tremendous difficulties, and the fortitude to reach inside and give your best even when faced with overwhelming odds. Heart involves strength and toughness. It involves leaders' awareness of their responsibilities to those they're entrusted to lead and the values of the organizations that select them. It involves forcefully imparting cherished values to those who look to them for leadership.

But heart, *cor,* has a double meaning. From its root also comes the word "cordial." Encouragement is about being generous and charitable.[5] It's about having a "big heart." When leaders encourage their constituents' hearts, they also show how profoundly grateful they are for the dedication and commitment others have shown to the cause.

Encouraging the heart, then, is about the dichotomous nature of leadership. It's about toughness and tenderness, guts and grace, firmness and fairness, fortitude and gratitude, passion and compassion. Leaders must have courage themselves, and they must impart it to others. This book is about how leaders effectively give of their hearts so that others may more fully develop and experience their own.

Who Should Read this Book?

As with our other books *The Leadership Challenge, Credibility, Everyday People, Extraordinary Leadership,* and *The Truth About Leadership,* this one is written to assist people in furthering their abilities to lead others in making extraordinary things happen. Whether you're in the public or private sector, whether you're an employee or volunteer, whether you're on the front lines or in the senior ranks, whether you're a student, a teacher, or a parent, we've written this book to help you develop your capacity to guide others to places they've never been before.

In this book, you'll find numerous examples of how ordinary people exercise leadership. What you don't find here are many examples of famous executives and celebrity leaders. It's not that they couldn't benefit from *Encouraging the Heart* or that they don't have wisdom to impart; it's just that they represent such a small percentage of the people who lead that they don't, and shouldn't, dominate our view of what leadership is and what leaders do. Most likely, you don't know or haven't heard about the people we report on in this book, but we're confident you know people like them in your workplace.

To us, *leadership is everyone's business*. Leadership is not about a position or a place. It's an attitude of experiencing a sense of responsibility for making a difference. Even if you don't consider yourself to be in a leadership role now, you may find yourself in one soon. *Encouraging the Heart* can be helpful to you as you prepare for that eventuality. In our studies of people functioning at their personal-best as leaders, we've written about people as young as nine and older than eighty who have assumed leadership roles. So don't count yourself out.

It's been our experience that leaders most often want answers to questions that begin with *How do I . . . ?* So we offer many how-to's in this book. We also intend to go beyond providing a prescriptive list of things to do. We want to offer you a set of principles that guide you in developing your own methods and techniques. That's where most of the fun is, anyway.

A Leader's Guide

Encouraging the Heart is designed to describe how leaders behave, explain the principles underlying their actions, provide many examples of leaders demonstrating these leadership practices, and offer suggestions on how to start being more encouraging. We've subtitled this book

Igniting Purpose and Providing Meaningful Recognition because we also make the point that genuine encouragement of individuals engaged in making extraordinary things happen needs to be linked to something greater than themselves—something that goes beyond extrinsic rewards and engages with intrinsic values.

The first three chapters introduce you to the basic message about encouraging the heart: the best leaders care. In Chapter 1, we present research to support this point of view, and in Chapter 2, we offer two case studies as illustrations of the seven essentials of encouraging the heart. Once you master these, you're on your way to becoming a caring and credible leader. Chapter 3 provides The Encouragement Index, an opportunity to self-assess the extent to which you believe you currently exhibit each of the essentials.

Chapters 4 through 10 explore the seven essentials in some detail. Although the discussions are built on our original and ongoing research, we expand this understanding of encouragement by drawing on the research of other scholars. Each essential is documented with numerous leadership examples.

Chapter 4 explains why encouraging the heart begins by being clear about standards aligned with purpose. Unless leaders and organizations articulate clear values and principles, it's hit-or-miss for colleagues when it comes to knowing the right things to do and why. It's also tough for leaders to know how to recognize performance when they don't know what to look for. Chapter 5 is about the leader's attitude toward others. Expecting the best is the only way we get the best, and this chapter tells us why and how "Pygmalion leaders" are the most effective.

When successful leaders expect the best, they're much more able to pay attention to what's happening around them and find examples of people living up to and exceeding expectations. As Chapter 6 shows, leaders always look for exemplars of values and standards. In Chapter 7, we learn the power of personalizing recognition. The best leaders get to know the recipient so that when it comes time to recognize, leaders understand how to make it special, meaningful, and memorable. Personalizing recognition is also how leaders communicate that they see and hear others.

In Chapter 8, we explain how great leaders are also great storytellers. Storytelling is one of humankind's oldest ways to communicate life's lessons and is an essential medium to broadcast and publicize stories of recognition. People learn best from those they can most relate to, so leaders use all available media to brag about people in their organizations who are living the values and performing at the highest levels. In Chapter 9, we show how leaders bring people together to share their colleagues' successes and provide the necessary support for one another. Social support is essential and indispensable to our well-being and productivity. Encouraging the heart is not about singling out superstars; instead, it's more about creating a sense of community in which everyone can contribute.

We conclude our discussion of the seven essentials by reiterating one of our consistent messages: leaders must do what they expect others to do. Chapter 10 is about how leaders must be credible, set an example, and create an environment for encouraging the heart. We summarize it all in Chapter 11 and note the importance of authenticity in what you say and do. In Chapter 12, we offer more than 101 ways to get started in your quest to encourage the hearts of your constituents.

In reading and applying the material in these chapters, we hope you'll realize that encouraging the heart is much more than being nice to people or acting like a stereotypical cheerleader. Encouraging the heart means employing a set of behaviors, principles, and practices that, taken together, add up to a powerful force in mobilizing people.

Keeping Hope Alive

We're living in a time of great promise. New developments in pharmaceuticals and biotechnology promise that some of the deadliest and most disabling diseases may be cured or at least better managed. New information technologies promise not only to connect us globally and create new forms of commerce but also to stimulate creativity, increase the speed of innovation, enhance productivity, enrich human experiences, expand information accessibility, and extend the reach of our educational systems.

At the same time, we're suffering from a severe hangover resulting from the deadly COVID-19 pandemic. Across the globe, many aspects of "normal" life have been upended. International tensions, including conflicts in the Middle East, Eastern Europe, and Africa, are making fewer of us feel as personally safe as we once did. Random acts of violence, mass shootings, and political incivility seem to be a regular part of the nightly news. Wildfires, heat domes, melting ice caps, and powerful tropical storms cause many of us to wonder when we're really going to hit bottom and if our lives will ever be the same again.

In today's fast-paced, seemingly nonstop, virtual, and visual world, getting caught up in the craziness can be easy. Slowing down and taking the time to encourage the heart is a major challenge. And yet, when matters are hectic and workloads are heaviest, people need to hear that they are appreciated for all their hard work and dedication.

But there can't be great promise without great hope. Bold leadership is required to keep hope alive, and *Encouraging the Heart* is ultimately about keeping hope alive. Leaders keep hope alive when they set high standards and genuinely express optimism about an individual's capacity to achieve them. They keep hope alive when they give feedback and publicly recognize a well-done job. They keep hope alive when they give their constituents the internal support that all human beings need to feel that they and their work are important and have meaning. They keep hope alive when they train and coach people to exceed their current capacities. Most importantly, leaders keep hope alive when they set an example. Nothing is more encouraging than seeing leaders practice what they preach.

These are tough times for many people. There's some apprehensiveness in our actions, a cynicism in our attitudes, and a creeping weariness in our bodies. The path to the future has always been full of challenges and opportunities, yet deep down, you and I know we'll get through these times—with courage and encouragement.

James M. Kouzes
Orinda, California

Barry Z. Posner
Berkeley, California

PART ONE

CHAPTER 1

The Heart of Leadership

Developing genuine gratitude involves carefully observing what employees are doing, walking in their shoes, developing greater empathy, and sincerely trying to understand the challenges they face. It is about seeing good things happening and then expressing heartfelt appreciation for the right behaviors.
—*ADRIAN GOSTICK and CHESTER ELSTON*
Leading with Gratitude

ASK YOURSELF THIS question: Do I need encouragement to perform at my best?

We've asked this question countless times in our leadership workshops, seminars, and classes, and at first the answers surprised us. Initially, we expected almost everyone to answer yes.

We were wrong. Less than half of the people we asked raised their hands, agreeing they needed encouragement to do their best. Puzzled, we asked them to tell us why.

They told us that they didn't *need* encouragement. After all, they weren't children anymore; they were adults and could do their best without being encouraged. They believed they could take personal initiative and responsibility without anyone cheering them along. Needing encouragement somehow implied that they couldn't perform well unless someone was around to praise them and tell them they were doing a good job.

These responses made us intensely curious. How could it be that research studies show that performance is higher among leaders who are more encouraging of others, and yet the majority of people were telling us they didn't *need* it?

Hmm. Perhaps we were asking the question the wrong way. So we reframed it: "When you get encouragement, does it help you perform at a higher level?" This time, nearly everyone said yes.

And then it was only a matter of logic to make the connection (remembering that in mathematics, if A = B, and B = C, then A must also equal C). If it's true that nearly everyone agrees that when they receive encouragement, it boosts their performance, then it must also be true that everyone *needs* encouragement. Of course, not everyone needs the same amount, variety, frequency, quality, or type of encouragement. But every leader who wants to improve performance and engagement must give it in some form. In the coming chapters of this book, you'll find empirical evidence to support this assertion. Simply put, encouraging others positively impacts them and the work they do.

Starved for Recognition and Purpose

Here's another question: "Do you like to be taken for granted?"

No one anywhere has ever raised their hand and said yes to this question. No one. So if no one likes to be taken for granted, and everyone needs encouragement to perform at their best, why do so many people think that positive affirmation is unnecessary?

One explanation is that people don't experience enough encouragement to realize its importance. Most employees don't get much recognition for a job well done, and most managers don't give it. With nearly two-thirds of Americans indicating that they never get recognized for outstanding individual performance, it is no surprise that almost four out of five employees who quit their jobs say that the failure of their management to recognize their performance—a lack of appreciation—was a major reason.[1]

Contrary to what employees report, 80 percent of employers cite compensation as why people leave their jobs. Yet only 12 percent of employees say that's why they quit. Some surveys have found that money comes in dead last when ranking the 23 most common motivators for leaving a position (true regardless of age).[2] Other studies find that employees who don't feel valued at work will leave for no pay increase.[3] One study found that if employees receive four or more "touchpoints" of positive feedback in a quarter, retention rates increase to 96 percent over the next year.[4] It's all about feeling seen and valued. People want their leaders to notice and acknowledge when they do excellent work. If they don't experience that, they're more likely to leave voluntarily.

For those employees who report the highest morale, more than 94 percent agree that their leaders are proficient at recognition. In contrast, only 2.4 percent of those with low morale indicate they have a manager who is great at recognition.[5] Meanwhile, the probability of great work is 18 times more likely when employees are recognized at work.[6] Companies that are most effective at recognition enjoy a return on equity (ROE) more than three times higher than the returns experienced by least effective firms.[7] And yet, while 50 percent of managers say they give recognition for high performance,[8] less than 20 percent of employees report that their supervisors express appreciation "more than occasionally."[9]

Think about it for a moment. You bust your butt to get that shipment out early or make the customer feel special, or invent a way to fix that troublesome glitch in the product, and you *never* get even a thank-you. This happens too often to too many of us—and even perhaps to all of us at one time or another. People need to feel appreciated by their managers and see that their efforts matter and that their work makes a difference. Otherwise, they wonder, "Why should I bother caring about my work?" "Does what I do matter to anyone?" "Should I show up today or just call it in (virtually or not)?"

Recognition ignites a sense of purpose and meaning in what and why people do what they do.[10] When people find a sense of purpose and meaning in what they do, they are two to six times more likely to stay with their company in the long term.[11] Research studies also reveal that employees' experience of meaning in their work is intrinsically linked to innovation.[12]

"Why should I provide recognition?" managers ask. After all, "Isn't this what we expect them to do?" "Aren't they just doing their job?" Or "Isn't this what we pay them to do?" Sometimes it also feels that "No one tells me I'm doing anything special, so why should I, in turn, tell anyone else that?" Or "I've never felt the need to have anyone tell me that I'm doing something special, so I assume the same is true for everyone else."

Paul Moran[13] echoed these sentiments at one time in his managerial career. "In the past," he told us, "I usually neglected to celebrate my team's accomplishments (and my own accomplishments) because I personally never placed much importance on this aspect of the job for myself. I tended to forget about recognizing the accomplishments of others. Rather, I treated their accomplishments as part of their normal job, which required no unique acknowledgment." Paul's reflection helps to explain why researchers find such a significant gap between how people expect to be recognized and acknowledged at work and their actual experience.[14]

When Paul left his job for a new position with a different company, he took another look at the importance he was giving to recognizing others and celebrating successes. On reflection, he realized that recognition made a difference to others in their relationships with him and their work responsibilities, so he decided to change his leadership practices. To remind himself of the importance of overt recognition, he developed a priority list of ways to recognize others. When his team achieved a key milestone, he would go around and personally shake the hand of every project team member.

He would take several key team members out to lunch and make phone calls to all members to thank them personally for their efforts in the project. He invited people to a small office party where cake and coffee were served.

Soon after implementing a more encouraging leadership approach, Paul saw productivity increase, absenteeism decrease, and a more robust human bond develop between coworkers and himself. Furthermore, his job became easier as individuals working with him began taking greater initiative. Fostering a more collaborative environment led to better communications, with fewer conflicts between staff members. While these celebrations and recognitions required a lot of extra effort, Paul felt that he should have done this earlier and more often in his career.

We can all do a lot more. We *must* do a lot more because if this issue is not addressed, both productivity and well-being will suffer considerably.

Opening Ourselves Up

There's more to explaining why we don't give and receive more encouragement than the assumption that it's part of the expected job performance. That's too easy an answer; it doesn't get to the root of the problem.

Expressing genuine appreciation for the efforts and successes of others means people have to show their emotions. You have to talk about your feelings in public. You have to make yourself vulnerable to others. For many of people—perhaps most—this can be uncomfortable, tough, and even terrifying.

Take the case of Joan Nicolo, a general manager with a financial services company. Encouraging the heart was particularly challenging because she was uncomfortable praising people publicly. Yet Joan knew her direct reports deserved and needed to be acknowledged for their work. Being a conscientious person who recognized that acknowledging others was an essential leadership skill, she started asking herself what was holding her back. On the surface, it seemed such a simple task, so what was the big deal?

After considerable soul-searching, Joan developed some theories about what she saw as shortcomings in her leadership abilities. For one, she feared others would think she was playing favorites if she praised one person. She also felt that praising and encouraging activities took too much time. It was just another item to add to her already burgeoning list of responsibilities. She was also worried that being a "cheerleader" perpetuated stereotypes of female managers and that people would view her as "warm and fuzzy," diminishing her reputation and competence. But the more she thought about it, the more she realized that her team deserved to be recognized and to know that she appreciated what they were bringing to the organization. She was determined to break through her resistance and try it.

At their next staff meeting, during a presentation, she made a particular point of thanking people publicly for fostering the collaborative spirit of the project they were working on. She told us that this simple action felt great to her and to others: "I found that my spirit was lifted. They felt appreciated, and I felt they had received the credit they deserved."

While Joan felt vulnerable opening herself up and thanking the group, she knew she'd established a human connection with her colleagues that hadn't been there before and would prove highly beneficial in the months ahead. Communication was more open afterward, people felt safer sharing their experiences, and even Joan felt far less guarded than ever before. This was a real turning point for her.

In the following weeks, she brought much more of herself to her work relationships, and people responded with a new level of enthusiasm for her leadership. She began to see all of the people with whom she worked in a different light. She could focus on getting the job done and enjoy a human bond with everyone around her. She felt more energetic than ever when she was in the office, and at the end of the workday, she felt increasing satisfaction with what she'd accomplished. At first, it wasn't clear how these changes would affect productivity. Would they translate into anything that benefited the company? In a relatively short time, she saw that this new way of relating brought her group together as never before, fueling an esprit de corps that spurred them on to give their personal best whenever an extraordinary effort was required.

Contrary to her worst fears, nobody got jealous when she praised one person or another, and the time it took to show her appreciation was well worth it. Summing up the experience, she said, "I learned that openly celebrating successes is essential to building and sustaining a unified team. Never again will I underrate the importance of encouraging the heart, of visibly appreciating others and their efforts in my future leadership experiences."

A Secret Revealed

We've all been deceiving ourselves for years, operating according to myths about leadership and management that have prevented us from seeing the truth.

First, there's the myth of rugged individualism. There's this belief that individualistic achievement gets us the best results. We seem content to believe that we don't need others to perform at our best.

The fact is, people don't do their best in isolation. Extraordinary things don't happen when people are isolated from each other. That's not how people make the best decisions, get the best grades, run faster, achieve the highest sales levels, invent breakthrough products, or live longer or more happily. Support, encouragement, expressions of confidence, and help from others are essential to achieving excellence.

We've also operated under the myth that leaders should be calm, aloof, and analytical; they should separate emotion from work. We're told that real leaders don't need love, affection, and friendship. "It's not a popularity contest" is a phrase we've all heard often, along with "I don't care if people like me. I want them to respect me."

Nonsense.

Think about that statement for a minute. "I don't care if people like me." Really? Exactly who are the people they don't care about? Is it family members? Friends? Neighbors? Colleagues at work? Managers? Direct reports? And if it's any of those people, then the person who doesn't care should never be in a leadership role. If they already are, then we guarantee that individual will never receive the best performance or the highest levels of engagement from their constituents. The best leaders want to be liked, and they want openness from other people. Not caring how others feel and think about who we are and what we do and say is an attitude for losers that can only lead to less and less effectiveness.

Leadership is a relationship, and the quality of that relationship matters significantly. In many of the personal-best cases we collected people felt that encouraging the heart was the most important leadership practice "precisely because it's the most personal." It's the practice that signals to people that you notice them. That you see them. That they matter to you. Leadership is all about people, and if you're going to lead people, you must care about them. People who feel you care about them are more likely to care about you. They are unlikely to care about you if they sense that you don't care about them. Period.

The Center for Creative Leadership (CCL) studied the executive selection process, and their results support the assertion that you must care. For example, in examining the critical variables for success for the top three jobs in large organizations, the number one success factor was "relationships with subordinates."[15]

The widespread assumption is that those in management positions need to express control. So you might think that would be the factor that distinguishes the highest from the lowest-performing managers. But that's *not* what the CCL researchers found.[16] Instead, the single factor differentiating the top from the bottom was higher scores on *affection*—both expressing and wanting it. Executives in the top quartile of a 360-degree instrument behaved in ways that helped create a more open, safe, and concerned environment with their subordinates and coworkers. They got closer to people and were significantly more open in sharing thoughts and feelings than their lower-performing counterparts. Executives with strong relationship skills create environments where people are motivated to do their best. The impact of these behaviors paid dividends throughout the organization, as the research showed that subordinates of the highest-performing managers *two levels down* in the organization were significantly more satisfied overall with their coworkers, supervision, top leaders, organization planning, ethics, and quality. Openness and affection clearly pay off.

Now, for the record, these managers were not without their rational sides. In fact, on another measure, they all scored high on "thinking" and their need to have power and influence over others. It's just that these characteristics didn't explain why managers were higher or lower performers.

These findings provide further evidence that the quality of the relationship between leaders and constituents is critical to workplace engagement and a leader's effectiveness. Leaders high in both dimensions of affection want to get to know the people around them, and they want their constituents to do the same. They want to understand others. They show they care. They show others that they're interested in them. They seek people out. They actively listen. They're considerate of others. They build rapport with others. They support others. They show their concern for others.

These needs and actions enable a leader to have more empathy for others. Empathy is the ability to understand and share another person's feelings, step into their mindset, and comprehend a situation from another's perspective. Empathy is essential for leaders because it increases trust, communication, and a sense of worth for team members. Daniel Goleman, the researcher who popularized the concept of *emotional intelligence* (EQ),[17] has said that of all the five dimensions of EQ, empathy is "the fundamental skill."[18]

Surveys by the accounting firm EY report that "empathy is not only a nice-to-have quality but the glue and accelerant for business transformation in the next era of business." The vast majority (88 percent) of respondents agreed that empathy leads to better leadership, inspires positive change within the workplace, enables trust among employees and leaders, and increases productivity. Their conclusion: "The modern workforce is crying out for empathy at the office—and if they don't find it, they'll seek it elsewhere."[19] What makes an empathetic workplace? We found that it's an environment that promotes positive feedback, recognition, and consistent appreciation. It's been shown that "when people feel regularly valued, they feel part of a workplace community. Healthy workplace communities make everyday habits out of giving praise and offering gratitude."[20]

The evidence is clear that expressing affection and demonstrating empathy are vital to success, and people have a high need for it. It's as if everyone is trying to hide something that everybody wants. As if there's a secret and if it were revealed it would make people look soft, wimpy, or who knows what. It should not be a secret that *everyone really wants to be loved.*

In our conversation with a veteran high-tech executive Irwin Federman, he eloquently expressed to us what we know from the data. He spoke an essential truth about the *chemistry* between great leaders and those who follow them. Irwin spoke of love as a necessary ingredient in leadership:

> You don't love someone because of who they are; you love them because of how they make you feel. This axiom applies equally in a company setting. Using words such as love and affection about business may seem inappropriate. Conventional wisdom has it that management is not a popularity contest. I contend, however, that all things being equal, we will work harder and more effectively for people we like. And we like them in direct proportion to how they make us feel.

Gary Burnison, CEO of the global consulting firm Korn Ferry, affirms what Irwin said. In reflecting on his decades of working with leaders around the world, he writes:

> For some, it comes down to two motivators—for love or for money. Money can rent loyalty, but it can't buy it. Love wins out every time. People want to be loved and they want to belong—and the most potent rewards address both of these desires. They can be done through a sincere congratulatory e-mail, recognition on the next Zoom conference, or even a simple "thank you." We can never say "I believe in you" too often.

I see you. I value you. You matter. You make a difference.
These powerful, affirming words mean one thing: you are
loved. At a time when we need to lead with heart, what more is
there to say?[21]

It's impossible to escape the message that if people work with leaders who encourage the heart, they feel better about themselves. Their
self-esteem goes up. These leaders set people's spirits free, often inspiring
them to become more than they ever thought possible. This, indeed, may
be the ultimate mission as leaders.

You will have to navigate and eventually cross a nebulous boundary
between yourself and your associates to awaken vitality in others. This will
not always be easy because most of us have been raised to believe that it's
crucial to maintain a buffer of "safety and good sense" between ourselves
and the people who choose to follow our leadership. One of the most significant risks you take as a leader is losing the interpersonal safety zone. If
you don't open up to others and express your affection and appreciation,
you stay safe behind the wall of rationality. However, the research demonstrates that it doesn't have to be either-or. You have a mind *and* a heart.
Both are meant to be used at work. You are more effective when you do. To
use your mind and not your heart is to deny yourself the greatest satisfaction and success.

Just Say Thank-You

Opening up is more challenging for some people than for others, but
significant psychotherapy is not required. It starts with what Robert Fulghum pointed out some years ago in his book *Everything I Ever Needed to
Know I Learned in Kindergarten*[22]: "Remember to say thank you!"

Study after study points out just how fundamental this phrase is.
For example, there's a significantly higher volume of thank-yous in the
most innovative companies than in low-innovation companies.[23] When
creativity is recognized and praised, the speed of innovation increases.[24]

Telling others their hard work and achievements are appreciated increases their willingness to continue putting forth more effort for longer than those who receive cash rewards.[25] Expressing gratitude also increases prosocial behavior, making people more willing to collaborate.[26]

When asked what skills their managers might develop to be more effective, employees place "the ability to recognize and acknowledge the contributions of others" at the top of the list. Data from thousands of leaders across multiple industries find that "every measure of morale, productivity, performance, customer satisfaction, and employee retention soars when managers regularly provide recognition."[27]

These findings are not new news. In 1949, a famous study by Lawrence Lindahl asked employees to rank the intangible rewards of their jobs. Then their managers were asked to rank what they believed the employees wanted.[28] The highest on the employees' lists were (1) feeling appreciated and (2) feeling that they were being informed about things happening. People wanted to be listened to. And what did their managers think this same group of employees wanted? They believed their employees would put good wages, job security, and advancement opportunities first. Most managers had no idea how highly their employees valued being appreciated and feeling informed and listened to.

You might say, "Well, that was more than seventy-five years ago, and much has changed in the decades since." We would certainly agree with you; a lot has changed. But a lot has not. Researchers have repeated Lindahl's study of employees and managers in the 1980s, 2000s, 2010s, and again in 2022. The findings have been remarkably similar each time.[29]

What about the managers themselves? What were they looking for in the workplace, and how did they rank these intangible rewards? Like the employees they supervised, managers ranked being appreciated, informed, and listened to as the highest on their lists. But why should this surprise us? Managers, leaders, employees: everyone is human and has needs to feel that they matter, believe that those they work with appreciate their contributions, and are important enough to be informed on what is going on.

In a series of surveys, we asked people to identify the most essential nonfinancial reward they receive at work. The most common answer was a simple thank you. Personal congratulations are ranked as the most potent nonfinancial motivators identified by employees.[30] Researchers also find that those who practice "gratitude" compared to those who do not "are healthier, more optimistic, more positive, and better able to cope with stress. They are also more alert, more energized, more resilient, more willing to offer support to others, more generous, and more likely to make progress toward important goals."[31]

Appreciation, acknowledgment, praise, a thank-you—some simple gesture that says, "I care about you and what you do." That's how you start. Whether in the form of a simple thank-you or an elaborate celebration, encouragement is feedback—positive feedback. It's information that communicates, "You're on the right track. You're doing really well. Thanks." To deny each other this gift of positive feedback is to deny increased opportunities for success.

Of course, there's more to it than this. The next chapter examines two cases illustrating the fundamentals of encouraging the heart. We also learn the fundamental principles essential to offering genuine encouragement to others.

As you read further, remember this chapter's essential message: Genuinely caring for people is at the heart of effective leadership.

CHAPTER 2

The Seven Essentials of Encouraging

Employee recognition is more than a nice-to-have—it's essential. When done right, it touches every critical element of employees' personal and professional lives and unlocks a powerful tool for leaders.

—GALLUP and WORKHUMAN
From "Thank You" to Thriving

WHILE PRESIDENT OF a manufacturing plant, Tom Melohn always enjoyed giving out Super Person of the Month awards to employees who went the extra mile to help the company achieve its goal of high quality and no product rejects. Tom made himself highly visible to everyone in the workplace. He presented the Super Person awards with a gregarious style that was his trademark. Because of his high level of engagement with the people around him, people felt they knew him. He put himself out there in person fearlessly, giving his leadership a little extra pizzazz, which tended to be mirrored back to him in the enthusiasm people brought to the workplace. Through the strength of his presence, Tom revealed that he knew what was happening, cared about people, got a great deal of pleasure from his work, and took pride in the accomplishments of others. He also ensured that people understood what was essential and the impact of their behaviors and actions.

Over the years, we've used Tom as one of our best-practices examples of how a leader can encourage the heart and, in doing so, promote meaning and purpose in the workplace. Consider what's being accomplished in this one specific incident that truly exemplifies all the essential principles and actions that form the foundation of this leadership practice. In this Super Person award ceremony description, pay particular attention to how Tom interacts with Kelly and "the gang," as Tom affectionately calls them, who have gathered to witness the award presentation. Notice the level of delight Tom expresses and how he engages everyone in the room through his questions and by adding dramatic elements to the celebration. Consider how he reminds people about why their work matters.

As you read this case example, what *essential principles* can you note? We'll be discussing them throughout the book.

> This scene takes place on the shop floor. Employees are gathered in the employee break area near the boxes and machinery of the plant for a Super Person of the Month award.[1]
>
> "We've got a new award today," Tom announces to the assembled group. "This month, we're calling it the Freezer Award. Now, who knows what that's for and who won it? Anybody? Anybody got an idea?"
>
> Somebody shouts out: "Kelly!"
>
> "There's something in the freezer," Tom says. "Kelly . . . go on, Kelly, look in the freezer. Go on. Come on. Hurry up!"
>
> Kelly opens the door of a freezer standing nearby and reaches inside. He finds a metal rod and cylinder, and an envelope is stuck to them.
>
> Tom laughs. "Come on up here."
>
> Everyone joins in the joy and laughter as Kelly walks up and Tom shakes his hand. Tom laughs some more, obviously

delighted with the fun the group is having at this ceremony. Tom takes the envelope and metal rod out of Kelly's hand.

"Oh, that's cold!" Tom exclaims. He returns the envelope to Kelly and sets the metal part on a table.

Kelly opens the envelope and pulls out a check.

"Okay?" Tom asks Kelly.

"Yeah!" Kelly says, smiling shyly.

"Remember this job?" Tom asks the group. "I went through the plant one day, and I saw Kelly going in the freezer. I thought, 'What the hell is going on? Is he goofing off or making margaritas, or what?' You know what he did? He couldn't get this (Tom points to the metal rod) into here (he points to the metal cylinder), so he said, 'Hey, I'm going to put this in the freezer. It'll shrink, and then I'll put the part together.' And it worked! And I said, 'Where did you get that idea?' He said, 'What? It's just part of the job, right?'" Tom looks at Kelly.

"Yep," Kelly says.

Then Tom turns to the group, holds the part in the air, and says with pride and caring in his voice, "And remember: no rejects, no rejects, no rejects! That's why we're here, gang."

What precisely did Tom do? What actions did he take? What words did he use? What nonverbal behaviors did he exhibit? What values did he exemplify that encouraged the heart? Here are some observations people make about this scene:

▶ Tom was genuine; he behaved like a real person.

▶ He personally saw Kelly do this while he was on the shop floor and took note of it.

▶ He showed that he believed in people.

▶ He cared about getting the "gang" (employees) together and made it fun.

▶ He recognized Kelly publicly, not behind a closed door in his office.

▶ He told a story about Kelly's actions, making them come alive.

▶ He didn't just talk about recognition; he participated in it.

▶ He gave out the award himself; he didn't delegate it to someone else.

▶ He was clear about the standards and how they were linked to achieve the purpose of total quality.

▶ He used repetition, repeating the standard "no rejects" several times.

▶ He used the part to illustrate Kelly's actions, making it tangible and real.

▶ He gave Kelly a check, sharing some of the organization's benefit from Kelly's action.

▶ He was laughing and having a good time, showing his enjoyment in recognizing Kelly.

▶ He got people together, ensuring that it wasn't just about Kelly but about Kelly being a role model for how everyone should think and behave.

▶ Tom reminded people why behavior like Kelly's was necessary; he inspired them.

As these observations illustrate, close analysis of the "Freezer Award" ceremony (and others like it) teaches that underlying the practice of encouraging the heart there is a set of recognizable, learnable, and repeatable actions leaders take that make people feel special, give them a reason to care, and reinforce the standards of the organization. After reviewing all of the observations we collected, we identified seven essentials to encouraging the heart. When leaders do their best to encourage the heart, they:

1. Set clear standards aligned with purpose
2. Expect the best
3. Pay attention
4. Personalize recognition
5. Tell the story
6. Celebrate together
7. Set the example

With the growth of hybrid and virtual workplaces and increasing globalization, some have wondered about the relevance of cases like Tom's, where everyone regularly comes to a plant, office, or workplace in person. If so, consider Cathy Warner's personal-best case of encouraging the heart.

As the business development manager for a multinational software company, Cathy has teams of people working worldwide, in the United States, Philippines, India, and Germany. Cathy used to work out of an office, but the company let the lease go, and now one of the bedrooms in her home serves as the office. She's hired everyone on the team but has never met them in person. Every week, she meets virtually with each one of the teams, and every other week, she convenes all the teams together (by the way, varying the actual meeting times so that for some it's morning, and for others it's afternoon or possibly evening). To reinforce a sense of togetherness, Cathy also asks everyone to share an update about something unique about where they are in the world at the start of every meeting.

Cathy makes a point to begin each meeting with "good news," calling out what various individuals and teams have accomplished toward their sales objectives. She'll often pinpoint the action by turning on a flashlight and shining it on the world map behind her to indicate "where in the world this good stuff is happening now." She'll ask one of her colleagues to describe the "good news," such as landing a new customer account or solving a key client's problem, and she'll share the lessons learned from making that sale with everyone else on the call during the meeting. Cathy's been known to conspire with someone on the local geographical team to surprise one of their colleagues with a small but tangible gift in recognition of a special event (e.g., birthday) or accomplishment (e.g., anniversary).

Cathy is always looking for "good news" from customers to share with the team and remind them about the higher meaning and purpose behind what they do (i.e., selling software). She regularly finds ways to emphasize how their products make a difference in the lives of others. Sometimes, these reminders come from their internal counterparts, like engineering, finance, legal, and so on. These latter messages reinforce the notion that the sales group is not an island in and of itself but connected with others in the corporation, with each department doing its best to make the whole enterprise successful. Maintaining solid relationships with other departments helps recognition flow both ways, too. Cathy finds out from these contacts if anyone has "good news" that she should pass along internally; for example, a new product feature provided by engineering is making customers happy, or the new billing process developed by finance means they can invoice customers more quickly than ever before. Cathy can't help smiling herself when, in meetings, team members comment on how her actions have made them proud, or more effective, or kept them in the information loop. Cathy's experiences encouraging the heart provide proof for the adage "what goes around, comes around."

Let's examine Tom's and Cathy's cases more closely to illuminate the essentials of encouraging the heart.

Set Clear Standards Aligned with Purpose

At the close of the Super Person of the Month ceremony, Tom said something crucial to understanding how to be most effective in encouraging the heart: "And remember: no rejects, no rejects, no rejects! That's why we're here, gang."

Tom had a clear set of standards that he expected people in the organization to live up to and the purpose for adhering to those standards. Whether walking the floor, making a presentation, talking to a customer, or holding a meeting, he and others knew the expectations. Most importantly, at the plant floor level, it was *no rejects!* None, zero, nada, not one. It was *why* they were in business. Anything less in the highly competitive market they served cut into their profits and threatened customer retention. For salespeople, like in Cathy's company, the standards are always crystal clear: this is what we must sell to meet our numbers and serve the customer's needs.

In recognizing individuals, it's easy to get caught up in the ceremonial aspects, but you need to remember to focus on substance. Recognitions are reminders; literally the word *recognize* comes from the Latin to "know again." Recognitions are opportunities to tell everyone, "I'd like to remind you again what's important around here. Here's what we value. Let me give you one example of how someone in this organization demonstrated what it means to meet or exceed our standards."

The first prerequisite to encouraging the heart is to set clear standards aligned with purpose. The standards were as much the focus of the "Freezer Award" as was the action that won Kelly his reward. In this entertaining moment, Tom linked the reward with the standards that had been set. The reward was for an action serving a clear purpose, just as Cathy would do in spreading the "good news." When Cathy spread the "good news," she wasn't just doing that to prop up her team—although it did. She also reinforced the standards and values she was fostering in her department.

Everyone must cherish a common set of standards to encourage the heart successfully. (We've chosen to use the word *standards* to mean goals, values, or principles.) It's certainly not very encouraging to be in the dark about what you're expected to achieve or never to know where you stand relative to what's essential. You can only set your sights on success when you know the standards and why they matter. By clearly defining the values and principles for which you're held accountable and by linking performance to those standards, you establish a benchmark for achievement.

However, not just any standards will do. They must be standards of excellence. They must be aspirational and bring out the best. They must make people feel like winners when they attain them. Indeed, "no rejects" is much more aspirational and inspirational than saying, "Let's see if we can get five out of ten right." Cathy's practice of spotlighting her team members to explain how the "good news" was obtained, just like Tom did with Kelly, connected strong performance to recognition. This signals that if one follows this behavioral model, other benefits follow.

Tom may have ended his presentation to Kelly with the statement about no rejects, but he also began with it—in his mind. Everyone knew what was expected, and repeating the standard at the end was just one more way of reinforcing the values that everyone, ahead of time, knew were important. Repetition is a powerful pedagogical device.

Standards are also crucial in establishing aspirations. The standards that leaders like Cathy and Tom set do not limit behavior and imagination. Instead, they offer a framework to help people envision and achieve their best—which is always beyond the current standard.

Expect the Best

Whenever we share Tom's case, people invariably comment on how genuine he is, how much he cares, and how much he believes that the people on the front line can attain a standard of no rejects and achieve zero waste and 100 percent quality. Talk with Cathy's teammates and you'll hear much of the same. The best leaders believe their people deserve the best, including the best leadership they can provide. They have an enduring belief in people's capabilities, almost always beyond the boundaries of any job description. They dedicate themselves to cultivating an environment where recognizing individual contributions fosters a culture of excellence and continuous improvement.

The best leaders believe that no matter their role, people can achieve the high standards set. This has been referred to as the Pygmalion effect, a belief so strong that even if others don't believe in themselves initially, the leader's belief—or the teacher's or parent's or colleague's—gives rise to self-confidence, to a belief that "Yes, I *can* do it." In essence, it creates a virtuous cycle, a self-fulfilling prophecy.

Belief in others' abilities is fundamental to encouraging the heart. Like it or not, your beliefs about people are broadcast in ways you're often unaware of. You give off specific cues that say to people either "You can do it, I know you can do it," or "There's no way you'll ever be able to do that." How can you expect someone to get extraordinary things done if they pick up the signal that you don't believe they can? Even if you said, "Thanks, great job," how genuinely would it be perceived?

As we describe later, when leaders expect people to achieve, they do. When they label people as underachievers, performance suffers. Passionately believing in people and expecting the best from them is another prerequisite to encouraging the heart.

Pay Attention

"I went through the plant one day," Tom tells the gang. This gives us an immediate clue as to the kind of leader he is. He's a wanderer, a walk-arounder, a leader who is right there with you. He's a leader in the truest sense of the word—a venturer. From the case scenario, we quickly learn that Tom is a leader who delights in "catching people doing things right."

But it's more than just *catching* people doing things right; it's also *paying attention* and understanding the significance of their actions.

All too often, people notice something happening but ignore it. They pass on by or file it away, thinking to themselves that they'll get to it later. Not Tom.

As Tom tells the story, he notices Kelly doing something unusual. At that point, he could have ignored what was going on. But being curious and because he cared, he didn't. Instead, he approached Kelly, started asking questions, and talked with him. Learning what Kelly was doing, Tom understood that this man's actions were the very embodiment of the standards the company wanted people to maintain. He was so impressed by Kelly's going the extra mile that he decided to make a positive example of him to the rest of the gang. By telling Kelly's story, he would encourage the heart of everyone there to align their work efforts to the value of no rejects. That kind of personal engagement is a genuine expression of caring. It helps foster trust and partnerships.

While Cathy had no plant or even an office location to walk around, she actively tried reaching out to people inside the company to learn about what her sales teams were doing that made a difference. Similarly, she kept her proverbial ear to the ground in talking with and meeting her teammates (even virtually), listening to and learning about what they were doing, what was working, what might be frustrating, and the like. She also paid attention to the many nonverbal cues available, even on screens, and even noticed whether or not people turned their screens on and what that might be communicating about their feelings. Listening and being present is a precursor to paying attention.

Leaders are always on the lookout for exemplars of the values and standards. Wherever they are, whatever they're doing, the best leaders have a special radar that picks up positive signals.

Personalize Recognition

Notice what Tom did to make this award memorable for Kelly. While the Super Person of the Month was a regular feature, Tom gave it a unique, attention-getting name: the Freezer Award, tying it specifically to something that Kelly—and nobody else—had done. Tom *personalized* it.

He customized the award and the ceremony just for Kelly—and he would strive to do the same for each "super person."

Tom didn't stand in front of the room and say, "Today, I want to present Kelly with an award for working to achieve the company standard of no rejects. Here's a check, Kelly. Thanks." Instead, he choreographed the whole thing. He put the metal part in the freezer so that when the time came, Kelly would return to it, open it, and take out the part. This is not something that happens every day. The fact that it was unusual, fun, and dramatic helps to imprint the event and the stated values in people's minds.

This emphasis on the individual uplifts Kelly and sends the message to others that singular efforts really can make a difference. We've learned repeatedly that people have become cynical about perfunctory thank-yous and run-of-the-mill award plaques. In too many instances, we've heard from people who received something of significant monetary value, yet because the leader hadn't put any thought into it and hadn't considered the *individual* who was being recognized, the effect was the opposite of what was intended. It didn't inspire the person to do their best; instead, it convinced them that the leader really didn't know or care about them. No one knew what surprise Cathy might be engineering for someone on the team. Still, they knew that Cathy was constantly looking out for "good news" to provide personalized recognition, not just for what they may have accomplished but as a way to honor who they were.

Before recognizing someone, the best leaders get to know them personally. They learn about their likes and dislikes, their needs and interests, and observe them in their settings. Then, when it comes time to recognize a particular person, they know how to make it unique, meaningful, and memorable.

Tell the Story

Storytelling is one of the oldest ways in the world to convey the values and ideals shared by a community. Before the written word, stories were the means for passing along the important lessons of life. We know how important they are in teaching children, but sometimes we forget how important they are to adults. Research tells us that stories have more of an impact on whether businesspeople believe information than do straight data.[2] Venture capitalists (some of the most numbers-driven people on the planet) always talk about how important "the story" is when taking a company public and selling the initial public offering to Wall Street.

The story is just as crucial to encouraging the heart. But why tell the story? Why not just bring Kelly up, give him the check and public recognition, and then have him sit down? Why take the time to reenact what was done? What difference does it make?

Well, let's see. Here's how the ceremony might have gone without the story.

> "We've got another Super Person award today," Tom announces. "Let's see, who won it? Uh, Kelly. Kelly won it. Come on up here, Kelly."
>
> Everyone watches passively as Kelly walks up to the front of the room. Tom hands Kelly the monthly Super Person plaque and a check.
>
> "Thank you, Kelly," Tom says matter-of-factly. "You showed us what implementing our zero defects policy means. Remember," he drones on, "no rejects, no rejects, no rejects!"

Yawn. Not only is this boring, but everyone, including Kelly, will forget about it the instant it's over. There's absolutely nothing memorable in this rendering. And it also doesn't provide Kelly's colleagues with a blueprint for success.

The intention of stories is more than to entertain. Oh, they're intended to do that for sure. But they're also designed to teach. The influential educator and philosopher Marshall McLuhan reportedly said, "Those who think there's a difference between education and entertainment don't know the first thing about either one."

Good stories move people. They touch us, they teach us, and they cause us to remember. They enable the listener to put the behavior in a natural context and understand what must be done to live up to expectations.

By telling the story in detail, Tom illustrated what *everyone,* not just Kelly, could do to live by the standard of no rejects. In effect, he said, "Whenever you encounter a situation like this, do as Kelly did. Kelly didn't want to waste even one part because we value zero rejects around here. So he thought about what he could do to live up to that standard. Everyone here can do the same in your job." Tom wanted people who faced similar opportunities to say to themselves, "Well, when Kelly was faced with that problem, he took personal initiative to find a solution. Now, let me see what I can do."

Besides giving context, good stories enable people to see themselves. You learn best from those you can relate to—individuals like yourself.[3] CEO stories might be good examples for other CEOs or those who aspire to that job, but they're not good examples for people on the shop floor. It's not that CEOs can't be good examples, but people don't easily relate to someone who's not like them. Besides, there's only one CEO per organization, while many more people are in other roles. People need to hear stories about those other individuals if they're going to learn how to behave.

Although the live example is the most powerful way to publicize what people do to exemplify values, other social media outlets are available. Consider creating a video of the recognition, sharing the example on Facebook or LinkedIn, and writing a story in the company newsletter, blog, website, or annual report. You could decide to feature someone's story or high-performance moments on your company's social media sites. You could create a practice of highlighting one colleague per week on social media. All of these, among other channels, can be used to encourage the heart and teach positive stories about what people do to exemplify shared values. These avenues are much more potent than posting or printing values on a wall or on the company's business cards. (Does anyone still use business cards?)

Celebrate Together

Cathy could have shared "good news" directly one-on-one with people, by email, voicemail, or video, but far more is achieved by recognizing people in public. Tom didn't simply call Kelly into his office and privately thank him. There's not as much to be gained by simply telling someone the "story" of what they did well in private; they generally already know what they did, although they may wonder if others know what they did. Having a story to tell is more for the benefit of others. This is how groups learn lessons. The public ceremony provides a setting for broadcasting the message and highlighting the behavior to a broader audience.

Many are reluctant to recognize people in public situations, perhaps fearing that it might cause jealousy or resentment. That's one of the things that initially prevented Joan Nicolo from doing more encouraging (as we saw in the preceding chapter). But if the leader is sincere, this doesn't happen. We asked one of Cathy's team members about being called out and receiving "good news," and she said it made her "feel great." She also told us how everyone is happy whenever someone gets this recognition. "Giving us opportunities to celebrate makes me feel more connected to my teammates and happier at work. It helps me notice things I appreciate in my colleagues, too," she said.

Most of people want others to know about their achievements, and the public ceremony does that, sparing them the need to go around bragging about themselves. Leaders who recognize others publicly have found that it rarely causes hard feelings and, in most cases, helps bring people closer.

Imagine for a moment that Tom does call Kelly into his office and gives the award privately. If Tom believes that doing so publicly will create jealousy among the workers, the scene might go something like this:

> "Kelly, I heard that you did something to help our efforts to achieve our goal of no rejects. To thank you for your initiative, here's a check for a hundred dollars."
>
> "Thanks," says Kelly. They shake hands, and as Kelly walks out the door, Tom stops him and says, "One more thing. Please don't tell anyone else you got this. It might cause friction on the floor, and we don't want that."

Kelly may have some extra bucks in his pocket, but he's also got a burden. He can't tell anyone. He can't be proud of himself and what he's done. He can't receive the high-fives and the "Way to go, Kelly!" congratulations. The opportunity to teach a valuable lesson by example has also been lost. This is no way to create an atmosphere of encouragement—just the opposite.

We see in Cathy's case and Tom's example that ceremonies of this kind are hardly frills or luxuries that you can dispense with in the workaday world. Today's leaders are discovering that encouraging the heart through public events builds trust and strengthens relationships in the workplace. By lifting people's spirits in this way, leaders heighten awareness of organizational expectations and humanize the values and standards so that they motivate at a deep and enduring level. Even more, public recognition serves as a valuable educational mechanism, demonstrating company values and encouraging others to duplicate the actions that they see rewarded.

Public ceremonies serve another powerful purpose. They bring people closer together. Leadership cannot be exercised from a distance. Remember what we said earlier. Leadership is a relationship, and relationships are formed only when people come into contact with each other. As we move to a more virtual world, where communication is frequently by voicemail, email, cell phone, and videoconference, it's becoming increasingly difficult for people to find opportunities to be together. Humans are social animals, and they need each other. Those who are fortunate enough to have lots of social support are healthier human beings than those who have little. Social support is essential to one's well-being and productivity. Celebrating together is one way people experience this vital support.[4]

Set the Example

You can't delegate encouraging the heart. Every leader in the organization—every person, in fact—must take the initiative to recognize individual contributions, celebrate team accomplishments, and create an atmosphere of confidence and support. It's not something you should wait around for others to do. "Do unto others as you would have them do unto you" clearly applies here. As we have documented in our other books, the foundation of leadership is credibility.[5] What is credibility behaviorally? Over and over again, people tell us credibility is "doing what you say you will do." Leaders *set the example* for others. They practice what they preach. If you want others to encourage the heart, you start by modeling it yourself.

That's certainly what Tom did. *He* set high standards. *He* believed in others. *He* paid attention to what people were doing. *He* personalized the recognition. *He* told the stories. *He* celebrated with others. *He* set the example. You must take the first step yourself if you expect others in the organization to follow your lead.

Tom also put his money where his mouth was in other ways. He made the recognition tangible by presenting Kelly with a check and putting Kelly's name on a plaque that went on public display. By themselves, the check and plaque didn't significantly contribute to sustaining the value of the action in people's minds. However, these tangible rewards helped memorialize the event when combined with all the rest. Though not a fortune, the money confirmed that the organization took the action seriously and was willing to share some of its gain with Kelly. The plaque reminded everyone that the organization values people who demonstrate behaviors consistent with the values and standards.

It may seem easy, but we have learned that encouraging the heart is among the most difficult of The Five Practices of Exemplary Leadership.[6] We find, for example, that leaders are more often seen by their direct reports as challenging the process or enabling others to act than they are seen as encouraging the heart. Yet the data also shows that those leaders who most frequently encourage the heart are assessed by their direct reports as the most effective leaders, as the ones they would strongly recommend to their colleagues as good leaders. Responses to the question "Where would you place this person as a leader relative to other leaders inside and outside your organization?" were directly correlated with the extent to which the leaders were observed encouraging the heart. Those leaders viewed by their direct reports as *very frequently* or *almost always* engaging in the leadership behaviors associated with Encourage the Heart were rated as "among the best."

We begin to see from all this that the seven essentials of encouraging the heart are vital leadership skills. They are not just about showing people they can win to make them feel good. Leadership is a curiously serious business. When striving to raise quality, rebuild after a disaster, recover from a global pandemic, start up a new service, transition to a game-changing technology, or make dramatic changes of any kind, leaders must make sure that people experience in their hearts that what they do matters. They must find meaning and purpose in their work, which in today's turbulent times can be difficult to experience and even more challenging to sustain unless one feels appreciated and valued.

Moving Forward

There's no better way to begin learning than to assess where you are now against some standard. It gives you a baseline for improvement. To provide you with that opportunity, we've elaborated on the encouraging-the-heart scale from our *Leadership Practices Inventory*[7] and created a twenty-one-item Leadership Encouragement Index (in the next chapter). By completing this brief survey, you can gain insight into the behaviors you are most comfortable with and opportunities for improvement by encouraging the heart. This assessment is intended to help you identify where to put your energy to produce the most remarkable improvements in the shortest period of time.

CHAPTER 3

The Leadership Encouragement Index

Pity the leader who is caught between unloving critics and uncritical lovers.

—JOHN GARDNER
On Leadership

WHEN RESEARCHING LEADERSHIP, we deliberately focus on how ordinary people, not celebrities with high visibility, lead others to make extraordinary things happen. We always want to know what people like you do to lead others to places they've never been. We find that most of us perform exceptional feats in our own lives and regularly inspire others.

Exemplary leadership doesn't derive from mystical qualities or inborn gifts but rather from individuals' capacity to know themselves—their strengths and their weaknesses—to learn from the feedback they receive in their daily lives, and to commit to continuously developing themselves—in short, their capacity for self-improvement.

Leadership scholars consistently note the high correlation between leadership skills and the capacity for self-improvement. The noted leadership scholar Warren Bennis pointed out:

> "Know thyself" is the inscription over the oracle at Delphi. And it's still the most difficult task any of us faces. But until you truly know yourself, your strengths and weaknesses, know what you want to do and why you want to do it, you cannot succeed in any but the most superficial sense of the word.[1]

More than four decades have passed since we began our work, and we've gathered volumes of information during that time. Our database has more than five thousand cases and five million survey responses. From all this data, we've concluded that leadership can be learned. Leadership development is self-development: getting feedback in your daily lives, setting self-improvement goals, learning from others and experience, changing how you do things to expand your ability continuously, and then getting more feedback to check our progress.

To know what to change in your life, you need to understand what you're doing that's getting the results you want and what you're doing that's not. It's essential to keep a positive perspective in mind. If you're in a leadership position or striving for such a role, the chances are excellent that you're doing so because you or someone else has recognized your leadership potential. To fully liberate that potential and put it into action, you need a pretty good picture of your strengths and how to build upon them.

To help you along the path of self-development, we created the Leadership Encouragement Index (LEI). The LEI expands on the essential behaviors taken from our Leadership Practices Inventory, which measures The Five Practices of Exemplary Leadership.[2] We strongly suggest you take a few minutes to assess yourself on the EI before learning more about the essentials. The LEI is strictly a self-evaluation, providing baseline information to expand your leadership skills.

The Leadership Encouragement Index

The Leadership Encouragement Index (Exhibit 3.1) lists twenty-one statements about what leaders do to encourage the heart. Read each statement carefully, then, using the ten-point scale, indicate how often you typically engage in each behavior. Evaluate yourself based on your present behavior—what you're doing right now—not from the vantage point of what you think you should be doing or what you'd like to be doing shortly.

Rate yourself numerically on each behavior by writing the appropriate number in the blank space to the left of each statement. For example, if you think you engage in the behavior "once in a while," write a 4. If you feel you "often" engage in the behavior, write a 7.

Note that you don't have to be in a management position or have direct reports to engage in these behaviors. Leadership, we like to remind you, is everyone's business.

Scoring The Leadership Encouragement Index

A rule in golf applies equally to self-improvement: *play it as it lies*. For you nongolfers, that means you have to play the ball from wherever it lands, whether in the rough or on the green ten inches from the cup. Applied to self-improvement, the notion suggests that you have to be able to identify and look very honestly at *where you are right now in terms of your skills*. The information you gather in this way tells you where to start improving, where to start building your skills, and how to make the most of your strengths. As every good navigator knows, you've got to see where you're starting, or the chances are good that you'll never reach your destination.

Exhibit 3.1 The Leadership Encouragement Index.

How frequently do you typically engage in each of the following behaviors? Write the number from the <u>10-point scale</u> below, and at the top of the next page, that best describes your response to each statement.

1	2	3	4	5
Almost never	Rarely	Seldom	Once in a while	Sometimes
6	7	8	9	10
Fairly often	Often	Often	Very often	Almost always

1. _____ I set a standard that motivates people to do better in the future than we are doing now.

2. _____ I express high expectations about what people are capable of accomplishing.

3. _____ I pay more attention to the positive than the negative things people do.

4. _____ I personally acknowledge people for their contributions.

5. _____ I tell stories about the notable achievements made by people I work with.

6. _____ I make sure that people in my group celebrate accomplishments together.

7. _____ I get personally involved when we recognize people's achievements.

8. _____ I remind people why what we are doing/producing is important.

9. _____ I let people know that I have confidence in their abilities.

10. _____ I spend a fair amount of time listening to people's needs and interests.

1	2	3	4	5
Almost never	Rarely	Seldom	Once in a while	Sometimes
6	7	8	9	10
Fairly often	Often	Often	Very often	Almost always

11. _____ I personalize recognition when I offer it to another person.

12. _____ I get to know people on a personal level.

13. _____ I hold special events to celebrate our successes.

14. _____ I show others, by my own example, how recognition should be given.

15. _____ I make it a point to offer feedback on how well people are performing against the standards we have agreed to.

16. _____ I express a positive outlook even when times are tough.

17. _____ I get to know the people I work with personally.

18. _____ I find ways to make my recognition of others unique and special.

19. _____ I recognize people for their achievements more publicly than privately.

20. _____ I ensure that recognition is aligned with our values.

21. _____ I congratulate individuals personally when they perform a job well done.

_____ TOTAL (Add together all the ratings above)

Once you've done the scoring at the bottom of the LEI, rank yourself according to the following explanations of your score.

From 186 to 210

You're doing great! You're probably seeing a lot of your associates producing at high levels. Morale is high. People like working with you because you keep the work environment upbeat and inspiring. They feel appreciated and good about the contribution they are making.

Encouraging the heart is a highly developed part of your leadership repertoire. Your presence alone is an asset. If you're not already doing it, look around for someone who could use your mentoring abilities to be as effective as you are at encouraging others. Also, if people aren't already taking the initiative to recognize and celebrate on their own, use your experiences and skills to provide structures and tools so they don't have to rely on you to get the ball rolling. Let them know it would be great if they, too, would encourage and celebrate others' achievements.

Finally, always look for new and creative ways to encourage the heart. Avoid becoming too repetitive, predictable, or boring.

From 126 to 185

You're doing pretty darn well. Although most of your colleagues are productive, you may feel they could be even more effective. Some grumbling might be present, but people are generally happy working with you. You may have the haunting feeling from time to time that there is something more you could be doing to motivate and encourage people, but you don't know exactly what it is.

You recognize that encouraging the heart is essential, yet you may feel reluctant to commit daily to this leadership practice. To take the next step, ask yourself what's holding you back from encouraging more. For example, some people limit how much they encourage others because they feel leaders must maintain a certain emotional distance from the people they manage. As you proceed, you'll discover you can maintain a certain distance even as you acknowledge individuals and celebrate your team's accomplishments.

Perhaps you're not the cheerleader type, and you're turned off by the idea of making too much of what people are getting paid to do; you feel that they shouldn't expect any special treatment. Even if there is some truth to this, people are social animals, and most respond well when they're acknowledged for their efforts.

Whatever the reasons you're holding back, take an honest look at them and weigh them against what you can gain by encouraging the heart. You might find that your uneasiness about this process fades away as you experience greater success and ease with this aspect of leadership.

From 66 to 125

People are probably not working to their highest potential, and a part of you is well aware of this fact. You might even feel that everyone is only working to capacity when they think you're watching them. Do not worry, though; there are plenty of tips in the remaining pages for you to put into action, and then you'll be well on your way to becoming more adept at encouraging the hearts of others.

You may feel there's value in encouraging the heart, but you're missing opportunities to implement the practice. Start paying attention to the achievements of the people around you that you feel are worthy of acknowledgment or celebration: a person going the extra mile to complete a project on time, a team within your organization completing a challenging task, or a person just doing something thoughtful that makes your job easier. Your recognition can include everything from a simple thank-you to an elaborate celebration.

If you feel reluctant to do any of this, see if you can identify what's holding you back. Lighten up! Think about things you can do to make your workplace more fun and inspiring to people who work there—and more fun and inspiring for you, too, we might add. Even a laugh or two can enhance productivity and worker satisfaction.

From 21 to 65

We guess that your score isn't this low. If it is, we hope you'll get busy applying this book's ideas immediately. If your score is this low, it's a good bet that there is a fair amount of discontent in the group or you're especially tough on yourself. The good news is that you can make immense changes that increase productivity and make your job much easier.

From our research, we know that most people produce more in an environment where they get positive feedback, and productivity diminishes where there is little or no feedback or where they only hear from their leaders if something needs to be fixed. Since it's your job as a leader to ensure people are earning their keep, you are probably not earning yours unless you encourage the heart.

Commit today to find something in your workplace to celebrate. Say thank you to someone who enables you to be a little more effective—and tell them so! Perhaps you don't appreciate how important encouraging the heart is for maintaining the vitality of your team. Or maybe you're just overlooking opportunities to celebrate and give recognition. See if there is someone else in your organization you can team up with to help encourage others. Find a role model and spend some time with that person as you learn from them how they encourage the heart.

Authentic leadership has intrinsic rewards; they come as you learn to work with others, not through intimidation and control but through cooperation and recognition.

Boosting Your Score

In the process of rating yourself, of course, you gain some insights into how much or how little you're encouraging the hearts of others, and you automatically get some ideas about ways to improve. For example, if you rated yourself low on question number 1, start looking for more opportunities to praise people. Low on number 5? Look for ways to celebrate accomplishments. In most cases, you don't have to leave the workplace to begin boosting your LEI rating as far as encouraging the heart is concerned.

As you move on to the following seven chapters in this book, you'll find lessons and positive examples of how actual leaders implement each of the seven essentials of encouraging the heart. Each chapter has examples, discussions, and suggestions for achieving the leadership goals described in this book. We do not intend for anyone to have mastered all seven essentials before bringing them into the workplace. On the contrary, new habits are built one small step at a time.

PART TWO

CHAPTER 4

The First Essential

Set Clear Standards Aligned with Purpose

The reason you recognize someone must be directly tied to the important goals and objectives of your organization.

—DAVID NOVAK
O Great One! A Little Story about the
Awesome Power of Recognition

TONY CODIANNI HAS worked in human development for most of his career. He loves people. He loves buying them presents, inviting them out on his boat, and cooking for them. Tony has nineteen first cousins, and he's taken them all to Italy. Ask the people who work with him, and they'll tell you they love to be around him. He makes them feel good.

But don't mistake his love of people for a willingness to forget about standards and the meaning of work. Tony says, "I always tell trainers in my group that they have to master the program first, and then they're free to change it." To Tony, having a clear set of expectations about what people will achieve is part and parcel of caring—and caring enough to ensure they know what it takes to meet and exceed the standards in delivering on their promises.

You probably read *Alice in Wonderland* by Lewis Carroll when you were young. Remember the croquet match? The one where flamingos were the mallets, playing card soldiers were the wickets, and hedgehogs were the balls? Remember how, in that match, all the pieces kept moving, and the rules kept changing constantly? Here's a refresher:

> "I don't think they play at all fairly," Alice began, in a rather complaining tone, "and they all quarrel so dreadfully one can't hear oneself speak—and they don't seem to have any rules in particular; at least, if there are, nobody attends to them—and you've no idea how confusing it is all the things being alive."[1]

Poor Alice became so frustrated. She had no way of knowing how to play the game to win. There seemed no reason to play; it lacked meaning and purpose. The game was also rigged in favor of the Queen of Hearts, and for the Queen, that was the point.

We've all been Alice at one time or another in our lives. Imagine one of those times when you've been unsure where you're supposed to go, what ground rules govern how you behave, how you're doing along the way, or even why you should care about what's happening. When you think you get the hang of it, someone higher up in the organization changes everything. This is a recipe for maddening frustration and pitiful performance. You just can't put your heart into it.

The first prerequisite for encouraging the heart is to *set clear standards aligned with purpose.* As we pointed out earlier, standards mean goals and values (or principles). They both relate to what's expected, but goals connote something shorter-term, whereas values and principles imply something more enduring. Typically, values and principles serve as the basis for goals; they define the arena in which goals and metrics must be set. When everyone is clear on the standards and why committing to them is essential for achieving a higher purpose beyond the tangible here-and-now of making money, it is easier to prioritize actions that directly create and deliver value. Being clear on standards helps people navigate competing demands and pressures and focus directly on what matters most. This also helps to empower people to know how to make decisions that are consistent with the purpose behind their day-to-day work.

Research shows that finding a purpose in what you do is more important to people than any other aspect of their jobs, including pay and rewards, opportunities for promotion, and working conditions.[2] People who experience their work as meaningful are more engaged, committed, productive, and fulfilled. And when people get regular recognition for their work, they will likely find it more meaningful. It's a way to acknowledge an individual's competence and signal that what they do matters.[3]

Purpose is the Glue

Organizational purpose can be defined as "an aspirational reason for being which inspires and provides a call to action for an organization and its partners and stakeholders and provides benefit to local and global society."[4] Surveys reveal that most executives believe purpose matters:

> Eighty-nine percent said a strong sense of collective purpose drives employee satisfaction; 84 percent said it can affect an organization's ability to transform, and 80 percent said it helps increase customer loyalty. . .but only a minority said their company currently runs in a purpose-driven way.[5]

People experience purpose when they strive or work toward something personally meaningful or valued. Most people say they have a purpose, although it may be difficult to identify or articulate.[6] Studies find that those people with a strong sense of purpose tend to be more resilient, especially in times of crisis. For example, research conducted during the pandemic compared people who said they were "living with purpose at work" with those who said they weren't. The former reported five times higher well-being and four times higher levels of engagement than the latter.[7]

Purpose is a feeling; beyond telling someone their work is impor-tant, you have to show them the impact of their work. Purpose is instilled when people can see that what they are doing makes a difference, and they have a personal sense that their contributions matter. People need to connect emotionally between a stated corporate purpose and their roles. You have to provide a line of sight that glues an individual's job to an organizational purpose, which enables everyone to see their part in the larger whole.[8]

One of the most effective strategies for helping people maintain a connection to purpose is articulating the "ripple effect" of their work, even for less-than-inspiring tasks.[9] The fast-paced nature of work and the complexities and interdependences of projects can result in myopia and a sense of putting out one fire after another. Enlarge people's line of sight by helping them see how their efforts impact others (the ripple effect). Help them look beyond their day-to-day tasks and reflect on prompts such as: What happens as a result of your output? Who is impacted by what you do, and how does that enable them to do what they need to do? What would happen if you stopped doing what you do altogether or slacked off significantly? While this conversation might feel a little awkward at first, people will be able to understand and appreciate that the things they are connected to have considerable impact.

Another strategy is to reframe the metrics associated with success.[10] People may feel a lack of purpose when they cannot assess performance or impact: "There's this larger purpose, and then there's my job, and I don't see how they are connected." Think about reframing success in terms of what people do. For example, instead of calculating the num-ber of customer calls handled or the average amount of time spent with each call, consider expressing this metric as the number of customers who were helped by talking with you. Rather than the number of new insurance policies written, measure success by the number of families you protect. This is more than semantics because framing numbers in terms of human impact creates significant emotional engagement. In addition, you can make sure that celebrations are linked with meeting the standards and fulfilling the purpose. People know what is important by what is celebrated, and we'll say more about this strategy in subsequent chapters.

Make Accomplishments Recognizable

Much can be learned about leadership from Girl Scouts and Scouting America (formerly known as Boy Scouts). We have personal experience with these organizations and have experienced firsthand their power of clear standards and recognition's role in honoring achievement.

In these organizations, boys and girls learn and pledge to uphold certain principles. Their deeds earn them advancement and recognition. As they achieve specific goals, they earn merit badges, and if they earn enough, they attain a defined rank. Recognition for achievement is a patch, a ribbon, a medal, or a pin.

But the nice part is that they wear them on their uniforms for all to see. Their peers know what they've accomplished and how they've earned it. It's probably no coincidence that people from scouting backgrounds, in proportion to their percentage of the general population, are more likely to serve in civilian leadership roles than people without that experience.[11] The merit badges don't make the difference, of course; instead, it's the standards and the discipline. The badges are the symbols of living up to the standards.

We've often fantasized about what it would be like to have this same tradition in adult organizations. What if you got a patch or a pin to wear every time you achieved a standard that signals to everyone what you've done?

This is happening in some places. For example, graduates of a leadership development program at a large publicly funded research lab started an "Action Consortium" to support their ongoing growth and development as they applied what they learned in the classroom to their jobs. The idea was that people would commit to furthering their development and taking on an action project that benefited the company.

Dan McDonald, one of the program's graduates, volunteered to chair the consortium. He borrowed a concept from his martial arts background to add extra meaning and uniqueness to the leadership development initiative. He used the idea of "pin progression" as a way to define seven levels of achievement. Just as colored belts in martial arts serve to signify levels of mastery, colored pins serve that purpose in the consortium:

1. White is the first level, and it signifies an *expression of interest* and a desire to develop oneself as a leader.

2. Orange, the second level, signifies the *beginning of the journey*. Earning it requires completing one program in the lab's "Leadership Alive" series.

3. Green signifies *growth*. To earn it, one must finish a second class and complete a project initiative with workgroup-wide impact in which aspects of effective leadership are evident.

4. Blue, the fourth level, signifies *nourishment* and requires completion of a division-wide project initiative in which leadership principles are demonstrated.

5. Brown signifies *a strong foundation*. To earn it, one must finish three leadership development classes, complete a project initiative with lab-wide impact (but limited scope), and demonstrate applying leadership principles effectively in the project.

6. Red denotes *passion,* at which level one has to complete a project initiative of lab-wide impact and moderate scope, again demonstrating the effective application of leadership principles.

7. Black is the top level; it signifies *service* and requires completion of a project initiative of lab-wide impact and complex scope. At this level, peers will regard one as a leadership role model.

This is an excellent example of creating a simple yet elegant way of connecting performance with rewards. They've defined each level and communicated what must be done to attain it; if standards are met, people can proudly wear their accomplishments—literally. Other analogous examples of providing a process for recognizing progress include more than two hundred organizations that have adopted a 12-step program toward recovery, various martial arts organizations using a color belt ranking system, and multiple branches of law enforcement and the military. Online sites such as LinkedIn allow users to showcase certifications they've earned. Some professional organizations have even partnered with digital badging apps to allow users who have attained professional accomplishments to display those credentials virtually—in email signatures, digital portfolios, and other places.

But how exactly do specific goals—the seven levels in this specific example—and values such as personal growth and service contribute to encouraging the heart? Sure, we know what they have to do with performance, but what part do standards play in uplifting people's spirits, imparting confidence, increasing optimism and hope, offering personal support, or boosting a sense of purpose? Let's take a look.

Commitment Flows from Personal Values

Humans don't put their hearts into something they don't believe in. You don't commit energy and intensity to something that's not a fit for you personally. Like wearing a pair of too-tight jeans, it's darned uncomfortable, you look awkward, you feel embarrassed, and you can't move around easily.

Our research shows that values make a difference in how people behave and feel about themselves, their colleagues, and their leaders. We know that people expect their leaders to stand for something, that they expect them to have the courage of their convictions, and that credibility is the foundation of leadership. The first step toward credibility as a leader is clarifying personal values.

The findings were quite thought-provoking when we took an even deeper look at the question of shared values—the congruence between personal and organizational values. Our studies, conducted over multiple decades, have demonstrated how strongly clarity of values influences a person's commitment to the organization's goals and objectives, especially the power of personal values clarity.[12]

In these studies, across multiple organizational settings and contexts, we examined the extent to which people were clear about (a) their personal values and (b) their organization's values. We placed respondents into one of four cells: [a] those with high clarity of organizational and low clarity of personal values, [b] high clarity of organizational and high clarity of personal values, [c] high clarity of personal and low clarity of organizational values, or [d] low clarity of personal and low clarity of organizational values. We also surveyed them about the extent to which they felt committed to the organization's goals and objectives.[13] Which of these four possible categories would you guess led to the highest levels of commitment to the organization?

The highest level of commitment is just where one would expect it to be. It is in the cell that indicated a high level of clarity about *both* personal and organizational values. Shared values do make a difference. The lowest levels of commitment are in the two cells indicating low clarity about personal values; this is true even when the respondents clearly understand what the *organization* stands for.

Finally, the second highest level of commitment is where there's high clarity about personal values but low clarity about organizational values. Though this surprised us initially, it makes sense because the individuals who are most clear on personal values are better prepared to make choices based on principles, including whether the organization's values fit with their principles.

Personal values matter most when committing to an organization. Different people are motivated by different things. As a leader, you must understand other people's core values to know what motivates *them*. If you don't live according to what you feel is essential, you will not give your all. A vital part of who you are is not engaged. You won't be working in a way that allows you to access your personal resources and abilities fully, and you will perform below your optimal levels.

It's extremely challenging to always put this knowledge into practice. Many organizations—perhaps even your own—send a team of executives off on a retreat to create a corporate values statement. They return with a credo in hand, print it on posters, laminate it on wallet cards, make videos about it, publish it in the annual report, hold training classes to orient people to it, and chisel it in stone in the headquarters lobby. Then they wait for commitment to soar. It doesn't. And it won't.

These efforts are probably a colossal waste of time and money *unless* there's also a concerted effort to help individuals understand their own values and examine how they fit with the organization. We aren't suggesting for one second that organizational values are unimportant. However, organizational values are only one side of the equation. Commitment is a matter of the fit between a person and an organization, and personal values drive that fit.

Jo Cheng, who works in the entertainment field, told us how she found it quite difficult to put her values front and center in her workplace. Jo told us that she initially struggled with speaking about meaning and purpose with others because she hadn't done her homework. That is, as she explained, "Since I did not know my own purpose at work, it felt like I was pretending or wearing someone else's shoes when I tried to convince my direct reports of the purpose of our team's work. Clearly, if I did not believe in what I was saying, I would not be able to speak with genuine conviction."

Jo is not alone in her experience. In Figure 4.1, the data shows the consequences of failing to genuinely connect with others about meaning and purpose at work—primarily that direct reports are unlikely to express much pride in their organization outside of the workplace unless their leaders consistently remind them of the higher purpose and significance of their work.

To create a sense of shared meaning and purpose, Jo had to start by answering for herself the question of "What gets me up in the morning?"

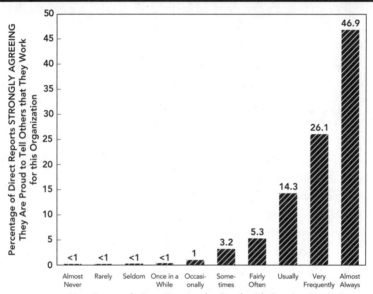

Figure 4.1 Pride is fostered when leaders frequently speak about meaning and purpose.

As she thought about what was exciting about her work and why she gets up every morning, Jo concluded:

> Entertainment is a fun and dynamic industry that can make work feel like being a kid again and getting to play on the world's best playground. I also realized that my work's magnitude of reach is beyond my imagination. Since I am responsible for bringing and promoting content to millions of users, any single project I work on can easily be seen and enjoyed by anywhere from thousands to millions of people.

Once Jo established her purpose at work, her conversation with her team changed when she reminded them of the purpose of "our" work. She found herself speaking with passion and conviction and able to paint a mental image of how their work reaches and is seen by fans worldwide. The data shows that the personal commitment of direct reports is directly proportional to the extent to which their leaders, like Jo, can bring their values to the workplace and find alignment with those of the organization. You must believe in what you are saying and doing and find ways for those around you to do the same. Recognition and celebrations facilitate this integration.

The implication for leaders is that a unified voice on values results from discovery and dialogue. Leaders must engage individuals in a discussion of what the values mean and how their personal beliefs and behaviors are influenced by what the organization stands for. Leaders must also be prepared to discuss values and expectations in recruiting, selecting, and orienting new members. It is better to explore early the fit between person and organization than to find out, late in some sleepless night, that there's serious disagreement over matters of principle.

Goals Concentrate Our Minds and Shape Who We are

Values set the stage for action. Goals release the energy necessary to act.

Many have studied the frame of mind called "flow," a highly focused mental state conducive to productivity. Flow experiences are when people feel pure enjoyment and effortlessness in what they do. Mihalyi (Mike) Csikszentmihalyi, considered the "father of flow," reported:

> In order to experience flow, it helps to have clear goals—not because it is achieving the goals that is necessarily important, but because without a goal it is difficult to concentrate and avoid distractions. Thus a mountain climber sets as her goal to reach the summit not because she has some deep desire to achieve it, but because the goal makes the experience of climbing possible. If it were not for the summit, the climb would become pointless ambling that leaves one restless and apathetic.[14]

Though many perceive goals as the finish line, Mike suggested that the critical function of goals is to get people moving with purpose and energy. Concentrating and focusing on something meaningful is most important to be at your best. By intending to do something, by setting a goal, you begin doing something. You act. The action you take has an intent. It's not aimless wandering; there's a purpose to your actions. You're not just marking time; you understand why you're doing what you're doing.

Goals also help you concentrate your mind and block out annoying distractions. They keep your eye on the prize. Voicemail, email, text, phone calls, social media notifications, mobile phone alerts, and shouts over the cubicle wall constantly disrupt your work. How do you know what to respond to? How do you know what to say yes or no to? Goals and intentions keep you on track. They tell you to put the phone in do-not-disturb mode, set the computer to sleep, close the door, and make the time to focus your mind.

Exemplary leaders ensure that work is not pointless ambling but purposeful action. Doing so helps people feel more alive, more in charge, and more significant. Goal setting affirms the person, and whether you realize it or not, contributes to what people think about themselves. "It is the goals that we pursue," explains Mike, "that will shape and determine the kind of self that we are to become. Without a consistent set of goals, it is difficult to develop a coherent self.. . .The goals one endorses also determine one's self-esteem."[15]

Is it better that individuals set their own goals, or should leaders set them for others? In the best of all worlds, people would set their own. Vast research proves that people feel best about themselves and what they do if they voluntarily do something. However, "people do not feel worst when what they do is obligatory"; they feel the worst "when what they do is motivated by not having anything else to do."[16]

You can relate to this, can't you? Remember when you were given make-work? After you completed a task, your manager couldn't figure anything else for you to do—or you didn't have the latitude to decide on your own—so they sent you to make photocopies to keep you busy.

Idleness is the devil's workshop and all that. The net effect is a stack of papers and a person who feels like just a pair of hands at the boss's disposal. The lesson for leaders is to be sure people know why doing something is meaningful and serves a purpose.

Goals Plus Feedback
Keep Us Engaged

People need to know whether they're making progress or marking time. Goals serve that function, but knowing you want to reach the summit is insufficient. You need to see if you're still climbing or are sliding downhill.

Research reveals that clear and positive communication significantly affects internal motivation and physical stamina. In one study, researchers wanted to find out how the presence or absence of goals and feedback influenced people's willingness to put forth the effort to perform a task. They found that motivation to increase productivity on a task increases only when people have a challenging goal *and* receive feedback on their progress.[17] Goals without feedback and feedback without goals have little effect on motivation.

Just announcing a quality goal of zero defects is not enough to get people to put forth their best efforts. Goals alone are insufficient unless you get some information along the way about how you're doing. Similarly, just giving feedback has no net effect. People ask, "Zero defects? Why are you giving me feedback about that? I didn't know that was our goal!" However, with clear goals and detailed feedback, people become self-corrective and more easily understand their place in the big picture. With feedback, they can also determine what help they need from others and who might benefit from their assistance. Under these conditions, they're willing to put forth more productive effort.

This result was well documented in a study involving soldiers who underwent several weeks of arduous training while competing for places in special units.[18] At the end of training, one final challenge remained: a forced march in full gear. The recruits' motivation was extremely high during the march; they knew that failure to maintain the pace during the forced march meant losing their chance to join the special units.

The soldiers were divided into four groups for the march, and there would be no communication between the groups during the march. Each group would march twenty kilometers (about twelve and a half miles) over the same terrain on the same day; the only variation was in the verbal instructions the groups received.

▶ The first group of soldiers were told the exact distance they would march—twenty kilometers—and were regularly informed of their progress along the way.

▶ The second group of soldiers were told only, "This is the long march you heard about." Nobody knew exactly how far they would march, nor were they informed of their progress along the way.

▶ In the third group, soldiers were told to march fifteen kilometers. However, after marching fourteen kilometers, they were told they had six more to finish.

▶ Soldiers in the fourth group were told they would march twenty-five kilometers. After marching fourteen, they were told they had six more to go.

Upon completion of the march, the four groups were assessed to determine which performed best and which group of soldiers endured the most stress. Which group do you think did the best and suffered the least from the stress of the march? Which group did the worst and suffered the most?

What did you guess?

The researchers found that the first group performed the best. Knowing how far they were going and getting regular reports were the keys to achieving the highest ratings.

As you might also expect, the second group performed the worst. Knowing only that "this is the long march you've been waiting for," not knowing how far they were to march, and receiving no information along the way generated poor results. Remember, these soldiers were in top condition and had completed the same training as group one. There was no difference in their group demographics. So the next time you hear something like, "Well, this is the challenge we've all been waiting for," watch out. It's time to ask for some more information.

What about the third and fourth groups of soldiers? Perhaps it's surprising that the third group of soldiers received the second-highest ratings. These soldiers were told they would march fifteen kilometers, but at fourteen kilometers, they were told they had another six kilometers to go. Apparently, for a highly motivated group, this was not as much of a letdown as group four's condition.

Group four finished third. They were told they would march twenty-five kilometers, but then, at fourteen, they were told they had six more to go. It's more of a letdown to think you have farther to go and then learn you have less than to discover you have more. It takes the proverbial spring out of your step.

Blood tests for stress indicators were taken during the march and twenty-four hours later; the findings corresponded with the results above. Specifically, blood was tested for cortisol and prolactin, hormones that rise with stress. Predictably, the highest levels were found in the group that knew the least about the march (group two). The lowest levels were found in the group that knew exactly how far they would go and received regular progress reports (group one).

Results from the forced march study and similar research tell us of life-enhancing capacities. At the very least, if leaders provide a clear sense of direction and provide feedback along the way, people are encouraged to reach inside and do their best. Leaders make the impossible possible and motivate people to strive to make the possible a reality. Clear communication about goals and your progress toward accomplishing them strongly influences your ability to achieve and how well and for how long you live. Talk about encouraging the heart!

Encouragement is Feedback

People hunger for feedback. They prefer to know how they are doing; no news has the same negative impact as bad news. Amy Johnson, an IT project manager, always made it a point to give her direct reports positive feedback; however, she was used to doing so only when they accomplished major milestones. She realized her silence in between major milestones equated to negative feedback. Waiting to recognize her team's contributions until after they accomplished major milestones was insufficient. She made sure in her one-on-one meetings with staff members to acknowledge what they had done and the positive impact they were making. She did the same with the group in team meetings.

Research on high-performing teams backs up Amy's experience. The positive-to-negative feedback ratio in the highest-performing teams is about six to one. Leaders of the highest-performing teams spend lots of time making sure the contributions of their peers are acknowledged and appreciated, reinforcing the sense of community in making extraordinary things happen. For moderate-performing teams, the positive-to-negative ratio is more like two-to-one. The lowest-performing groups spend most of their time and effort pointing fingers at their colleagues' inadequacies and blaming others as the reason they couldn't get their work done. Indeed, in these groups, there are almost three times the number of negative comments versus positive ones.[19]

Encouragement is a tangible form of feedback. It's positive information that tells you that your efforts and work are being noticed, and you are making progress, on the right track, and living up to the standards. The wonderful thing about encouragement is that it's more personal than other feedback forms.

Encouragement requires leaders to get close to people. It shows that you care about them and demonstrates that you are interested in more than just yourself. Because it's more personal and positive, encouragement is more likely to accomplish something other feedback forms cannot. Encouraging the heart strengthens trust between leaders and their constituents, a relationship critical to making extraordinary things happen in organizations. Encouraging the heart accomplishes something else essential to excellence. It speaks to people's hearts—to deeply held values and beliefs, to something beyond the material—and contributes to creating meaning in the workplace.

There's a deep human yearning to make a difference. People want to commit to and unite in a common cause where they can accomplish extraordinary things. Great leaders, like great organizations, create *meaning*, not just wealth.

The most admired leaders in every walk of life know that the first essential for enlisting others is to identify and emphasize the shared values of a culture—and understand what it means to the members. This communion of purpose helps bring people together, strengthen relationships, and create a tighter knit community. The best leaders can bring out and nurture this human longing for meaning and fulfillment. When leaders unequivocally communicate clear standards, they honor everyone's desire to achieve their best. They elevate the human spirit.

However, to ensure that people achieve their best, leaders must bring forth the best from others. Bringing forth the best begins with believing in the best possibilities, which becomes a self-fulfilling prophecy.

REFLECT ON
SETTING CLEAR STANDARDS ALIGNED WITH PURPOSE

Ask Yourself:

1. What values and principles do I most cherish?
2. How am I communicating these beliefs to others? How clear are others about what I stand for?
3. Am I creating meaning at work beyond just making money?
4. What does success look like? What does it feel like?
5. Am I setting clear goals and giving regular feedback on the progress toward those goals?
6. How effective am I at connecting people's daily actions to the larger purpose of our work and infusing their work with meaning?
7. What can I do to get feedback on how my actions impact others?

CHAPTER 5

The Second Essential

Expect the Best

I may be one of the most naïve people on the planet. I've always assumed people are trying their best. Sometimes I get disappointed, but I'm okay with that because I think it's so much more healthy that way than assuming the worst.

—HUBERT JOLY
Former Chairman and CEO, Best Buy

IN GREEK MYTHOLOGY, there is a legendary story about Pygmalion, a sculptor who carves an ivory alabaster statue of a beautiful woman and finds it so perfect that he falls in love with it. He is so enamored of his creation that he spends all his time gazing at her and thinking about her. He longs to bring her to life but knows that, alas, she is only made of stone. Heartsick, the yearning Pygmalion summons Aphrodite, the goddess of beauty, love, and fertility. He pleads with her to bring his beautiful statue to life. Aphrodite grants the sculptor his wish and gives the statue life. Pygmalion, of course, is overjoyed.[1]

Playwright George Bernard Shaw wrote *Pygmalion* for the stage based on this classic tale. You may remember it as the musical *My Fair Lady*. In it, Professor Henry Higgins, a phonetics teacher, meets an ill-spoken Cockney flower girl named Eliza Doolittle. Higgins believes he can, by the force of his skill and will, transform the flower girl into a lady. His efforts and Doolittle's courage and persistence lead to her transformation. The results are more than playacting. Not only does she learn to speak and act like a lady, but Eliza Doolittle becomes one inside. She learns to believe in herself.

Social and behavioral scientists began to apply the lessons of this legendary story to classrooms and the workplace. The phrase "self-fulfilling prophecy" theorized that when a person predicts that something will occur, their expectation changes how the person behaves. The changed behaviors make the event more likely to happen.

Harvard professor Robert Rosenthal extensively tested this theory, coining the term "Pygmalion effect" during one of his experiments to explain what occurred.[2] He and other researchers have documented that if the expectation is that someone will succeed, they probably will. If the expectation is that someone will fail, they probably will. People tend to live up or down to the expectations of them. Hundreds of research studies have since been conducted to test this notion, and they all demonstrate that people tend to act consistently with what is expected of them.[3]

If you have someone who believes in you and constantly reinforces that belief through their interactions with you, you will be strongly influenced by that support. If the potential exists within an individual, it comes out when a leader takes the time to bring them along. Leaders communicate expectations in many ways. Leaders with positive expectations set a climate that makes people feel more at ease. They offer positive reinforcement, share information, give opportunities for input, provide additional resources, lend assistance, and offer better assignments. Those with negative expectations behave the opposite. Now, it doesn't seem that hard to surmise which behavioral set will produce better results. The leader's attitude influences their behavior toward others, and that behavior influences the results.

Even more important, researchers have found that as people learn, they can perform in innovative ways, and they begin to develop expectations of themselves. Their self-prophecies become self-fulfilling. As Jody Chock, senior manager in the consumer goods industry, observed, "Folks have to believe that they can handle challenges and solve problems, or they won't even try. Indeed, they probably can't without believing in themselves and their own capabilities." This phenomenon doesn't just apply to the leader-employee relationship: A person will believe in themselves more if a coworker they respect believes in them.

Leaders uplift people's spirits and arouse their internal drive and commitment. They do this by believing in their constituents' abilities and putting their faith in them. What happens when someone says, "I have confidence in you, and I am sure you are the right person to do this job"? People get motivated to do their best to keep up with those expectations.

Jody notes that what characterizes leaders "is that they absolutely maintain high expectations regarding what individuals and teams can accomplish and are constantly striving for more." He adds, "Even in the worst news, a ray of light can be found, and being positive sets the tone, improves relationships, and ultimately, the business outcome." Exemplary leaders know that the combination of high expectations and positive reinforcement drives achievement and fosters a culture of motivation, collaboration, and innovation.

Common sense, right? Would any managers in their right mind think or act differently? Yet researchers have found that managers "accidentally and usually with the best intentions—are often complicit in an employee's lack of success. How? Creating and reinforcing a dynamic essentially sets up perceived under-performers to fail."[4]

The set-up-to-fail syndrome (a counterpoint to the Pygmalion effect) can begin innocently. It can start when managers distance themselves from a direct report for personal reasons. Or perhaps an employee seems to have a performance problem—a missed deadline or a lost account. This triggers an increase in the manager's micro-supervision of that person, who, in turn, begins to believe that their manager lacks trust and confidence in them. Eventually, because of these low expectations, the employee withdraws, stops making independent decisions, avoids risks, and ceases taking initiative. This reinforces the manager's original assessment that the individual is a poor performer and the problem intensifies. This set-up-to-fail syndrome, researchers conclude:

> is self-fulfilling and self-reinforcing—it is the quintessential vicious circle. The process is self-fulfilling because the boss's actions contribute to the very behavior that is expected from weak performers. It is self-reinforcing because the boss's low expectations, in being fulfilled by his subordinates, trigger more of the same behavior on his part, which in turn triggers more of the same behavior on the part of the subordinate.[5]

While both high and low expectations influence other people's performance, only high expectations positively impact actions and feelings about oneself. Only high expectations can encourage the heart.

High Expectations Lead to High Performance

One of our graduate students, Andrea Frankson, recently calculated that "over the course of our lives, assuming a forty-hour work week, we will likely spend over eighty thousand hours at work" and concluded, "Good leadership makes those hours feel purposeful." She contended, "It is rare to meet someone who has never dealt with a bad manager," and told us how she had to deal with a "bad manager" on her first job following graduation, who exhibited many destructive behaviors. This person:

mostly treated me as if I was a cog in a machine. I was told my work was good, but it did not matter—that the quality of my work was less important than my newcomer status at the organization. I needed to put in my time, which would pay off one day. I sulked at work each day and counted down the minutes until the end of the day. My coworkers and I bonded over our distaste for our manager, who was clueless and treated everyone as if they were overdue for a mistake. We never strived to improve or put in extra work because expectations were set so low. Negative feedback was given publicly and harshly.

Over the course of her career, Andrea has learned that the most effective leaders have high expectations, both of themselves and their constituents. These expectations aren't just *fluff* that they hold in mind to keep a positive outlook or psych themselves up. Another person's belief in our abilities accomplishes much more than that. Exemplary leaders' expectations provide the framework into which people fit their own realities. As with the Pygmalion effect, the framework plays a vital role in developing people. Maybe you can't turn a statue into an actual person, but you can release the highest potential of your constituents.

Nancy Tivol, a community services agency executive director, is a wonderful example of this principle in action. She believes strongly in her abilities and those of every staff member and volunteer. When Nancy came on board, volunteers were, in her opinion, underused. Many board members and paid staff felt that volunteers didn't have the skills to handle interactions with clients, donors, and corporate contacts. However, Nancy believed they could, so she started assigning more skill-heavy tasks to volunteers as opportunities arose. These days, volunteers are doing things that only staff members did previously. Indeed, more than seven hundred volunteers run the front office, the agency's three food programs, the Community Christmas Center, the agency's computer operations, and the Volunteer Language Bank—all under one director of volunteers. Most of the lead volunteers are more than sixty-five years of age. Volunteer hours increased from six thousand to twenty thousand annually, which enabled paid staff to be reduced through attrition from fifteen to eleven people. Not only that, but they became the only emergency assistance agency that has not turned eligible clients away because available funds were depleted. Under her leadership, the agency increased its funding for the emergency assistance program for low-income families during the pandemic—a period in which many agencies experienced significant funding cutbacks!

Previous administrators, as well as paid staff, had made certain assumptions about volunteers. They assumed that because they were volunteers, they would be neither motivated nor skilled nor experienced enough to take on the responsibility that some of the tasks at the agency would require. As a result, volunteers were mainly employed at jobs that demanded very little of them and were given only minimal responsibilities. The bottom line was that they were never given the opportunity to explore or demonstrate their capacities beyond the performance of the most menial tasks. Their beliefs, their *prophecies*, as it were, held the volunteers back; Nancy's beliefs encouraged the same group of people to excel. She placed volunteers in responsible positions, gave them the required training and direction, and encouraged them to do their best. And they did just that!

For example, when it became evident that they would need to upgrade their computer system, the assumption was that there wasn't enough money to set up the new system and train people. Nancy saw this not as an obstacle but as an opportunity. Once again, she turned to volunteers—entrusting the job to her fifteen-year-old son, a computer whiz who found the prospect a real challenge. For his Eagle Scout project, he wrote a forty-one-page manual on the new system he had coded. Then he trained ten Boy Scouts from his troop to become "coaches," who taught others in the agency how to use the new computer system. Each scout adopted a staff member or volunteer and stood by them as they learned the system.

Why did the organization change so radically under Nancy's leadership? The key was that she had very high *expectations* of her volunteers, who breathed new life into the people around her. She prophesied their success.

Our research shows that people are often anxious or nervous when they are encouraged by people in leadership positions to deliver their personal best. But at the same time, when leaders held high expectations for them, they rose to the challenge: they marched in, moved forward, and did what was expected without hesitation. All those we interviewed were willing and excited by the challenges they faced. Spurred on by their leaders' high expectations, they developed the self-confidence that gave them the courage and volition to live up to their leaders' expectations. These sentiments were evident when Ken Nicol described one of his earliest experiences in the construction industry:

> I recall my supervisor (Martin) constantly telling me I had more capabilities than I believed. This was quite uplifting, and when I was faced with obstacles, it kept me motivated to overcome them. Martin had this ability to make people believe they could do anything.
>
> On one job walk with Martin, he told me I would be the lead engineer for an upcoming large-scale project. I had never had such a responsibility in the company before and inevitably questioned my ability to handle this assignment. I voiced my concerns with Martin; he couldn't have responded better. He proceeded to list some of my strong attributes and recognized some efforts I had made in the past, connecting them to the skills I'd utilize with this project. It was quite clear he believed I could do this project—and with high quality. When the project was finally completed, he approached me and exclaimed, 'See, I told you that you could do it!' His recognition and belief in me made me want to tackle any upcoming projects that may be out of my realm. I learned a lot about myself and what I could do because of the high standards and expectations he had for me.

This demonstration of belief in another's abilities doesn't only occur in organizational settings. It can show up anywhere. A moving and powerful instance comes from Idaho businessman Don Bennett. Don was the first amputee to climb Mt. Rainier's summit—14,408 feet on one leg and two crutches![6]

During a rugged portion of the climb, Don and his team had to cross an ice field. To get across the ice, the climbers had to put crampons on their boots to prevent slipping and to dig into the ice for leverage and stability. Unfortunately, with only one cramped boot and two crutches, Don would get stuck in the ice. The only way he could figure to get across the ice field was to fall face forward onto the ice, pull himself as far forward as he could, stand up, and then fall forward again. Getting across the ice field would seemingly require a lot of faceplants.

His young teenage daughter, Kathy, was with him on this climb, and she saw what was happening to her dad. The team leader also noticed, and he began cutting holes in the ice so Don could hop into the clear snow and traverse the ice field. Kathy stayed by his side and shouted in his ear: "You can do it, Dad. You're the best dad in the world. You can do it, Dad!"

Over this four-hour struggle, Don knew there was no way he would have made it across that ice field without his daughter's encouragement. What Kathy did was leadership. Her belief in her father and her verbal encouragement touched a place deep within Don, strengthening his resolve and commitment.

Positive Images Create Positive Possibilities

Positive expectations yield positive results. They create positive mental images yielding other positive possibilities. Positive futures for self and others are first constructed in the mind. Seeing is believing, and the results can be life-affirming and life-enhancing.

Athletes have known for a long time that stored mental pictures influence performance. Unless a person can see themselves as successful, producing the behavior that leads to success is tough. Experiment after experiment shows that positive images make people and groups more effective, relieve symptoms of illness, and enhance achievement in such varied settings as school, the military, and business.[7]

One fascinating experiment involved people learning to bowl, demonstrating the power of positive images on performance. Divided into different groups, sets of bowlers were first instructed in effective bowling methods. Following these lessons, the bowlers were videotaped while practicing. One group of the videotaped bowlers saw only the positive things they did, and the other saw only the negative. Those who saw only their positive moves improved significantly more than any of the other bowlers.[8]

Dutch sociologist Fred Polak has observed that "the rise and fall of images of the future precedes or accompanies the rise and fall of cultures. As long as a society's image is positive and flourishing, the flower of culture is in full bloom. Once the image begins to decay and lose its vitality, however, the culture does not long survive."[9]

There is profound truth in this observation. Take a look around your organization, your community, and your neighborhood. Are the images and the stories told positive or negative? What does this portend? Is your organization's culture in ascendance or decay? Given the increasing cynicism of the workforce and the growing distrust of large organizations and governments, one might legitimately wonder what the future holds. As individuals and leaders, you must begin to paint more affirmative images for yourself and your constituents if you want to encourage others to commit to positive actions.

Fostering positive expectations is also a deterrent to "stereotype threat," similar in many ways to the often-called "imposter syndrome." Negative stereotypes can impair performance because to be successful on a job, people need to feel they belong there, are accepted and valued, and have the skills and inner resources to be successful. When negative stereotypes undermine these assumptions, they hamper performance.[10]

In one set of studies, men and women who were strong in math were recruited to solve problems from the qualifying exam for graduate school.[11] They took the test in two groups, with the first told the test usually showed differences in ability between men and women. In contrast, the second group was told nothing about gender differences. The women's scores on the test were appreciably lower than the men's, but only in the first group, where they had been told that the test was sensitive to gender differences. In the second group, where they were not reminded about gender issues, women did as well as men on the test. This same performance-lowering effect occurred when Black test takers were given a similarly threatening message. The active ingredient in lowering women's scores, or those of Black test takers, was debilitating anxiety. Though they had the potential to perform well, the anxiety triggered by the threatening negative stereotype or feeling that they were somehow imposters in the situation impaired their performance. Those most likely to feel these effects are those at the vanguard of a group, for example, the first LGBTQ+ or trans group members to enter a law firm. At this point, people are particularly vulnerable to doubting their abilities, questioning their talents and skills, and thus undermining their sense of capability. Their anxiety acts as a spotlight, both for themselves and (at least in their minds) for those who are watching to see how well, or how poorly, they will do.

Positive expectations and images generally reflect a meritocracy in leaders' minds and a strong respect and appreciation for people from different backgrounds and experiences. The Pygmalion within leaders sees the possibilities for greatness within each team member. Success through others, recognizing that extraordinary achievements require the commitment and cooperation of other (and often many) people, means that leaders must bring positive expectations to every workplace site. They must value the insights people of diverse backgrounds bring to the workplace.

Building Confidence
As Well As Competence

It's evident that just as leaders' high expectations can have a Pygmalion effect on their constituents, the expectations of constituents can also influence the behavior of their leaders. It has been shown that when constituents communicate high expectations of how good a person can be as a leader, that individual will likely adjust their self-concept and self-expectations to match what others think of them. With this motivation for exemplary leadership behavior, the constituents' prophecy is fulfilled.

It is no wonder that when people (like Ken Nichol previously) tell us about the leaders who made a difference in their lives, they frequently tell us about people who believed in them and encouraged them to reach beyond their self-doubts to realize their most significant strengths fully. They talk about leaders who treated them in ways that buoyed their self-confidence, making it possible for them to achieve more than they initially believed they could.

Expecting the best of self and others is not just some warmed-over version of the power of positive thinking. Because exemplary leaders have a growth mindset, they believe people can learn and develop. They are willing to exert the effort and provide the resources for people to do just that. Leaders with a fixed mindset, who believe that they as well as others have innate abilities that are not amenable to change, fail to take advantage of opportunities for improvement. Remember that experiment with bowlers we just mentioned? Those who believed they could improve continued to practice and got better, while those who thought they were not very good at bowling showed little interest and motivation to improve.

In a seminar or classroom, we often ask people how many would like to have more confidence due to being in the session. Almost all hands go up. "Okay," we say, "we'll make you a counteroffer. We're not going to promise to give you more confidence. We're going to promise to provide you with more competence. And then we'll ask you to see where confidence comes from."

Then we ask how many of them think of confidence as a prerequisite; that is, by a show of hands, how many will do something if they feel confident enough to do it. All of the hands go up. Next, we ask them what they are confident about in their lives and how they got to be confident about those things. Whether it's horseback riding, shipping products, or writing software code, they all became confident by repeatedly doing something and getting better with practice. Oh, so then confidence is an aftermath, not a prerequisite.

Then it hits them. They've been waiting their whole lives to be confident before trying to do something new when they couldn't possibly be confident until they were competent. This realization is transformational. It suddenly sheds light on whole arenas of restriction and impediment for people, which have nothing to do with anything other than the context from which they perceive the situation or themselves.

Exemplary leaders build competence by being self-confident and believing people can develop and grow. Because they believe people can learn and grow, they give them the opportunities to do so and, in the process, strengthen people's confidence in their own abilities to make a difference. You can't do what you don't know how to do until you get the chance to try to do it. The origin of most people's personal-best as leaders was the opportunity to do something they had never done or achieved before, coupled with the belief that they could be successful.

Our data shows that 97 percent of those direct reports who strongly agree that they are "personally effective" also indicate that their leaders very frequently or always "ensure people grow in their jobs by learning new skills and developing themselves." The results are very similar when asked how strongly people feel valued in their workplace, with a positive correlation to their leaders building their competence and confidence. The data in Figure 5.1 shows that direct reports most strongly agree that the leaders they work with "have their best interests at heart" in direct proportion to how frequently they observe their leaders taking actions that ensure "people grow in their jobs by learning new skills and developing themselves."

Building competence and confidence demands an organizational culture conducive to learning, and a prime prerequisite is an environment,

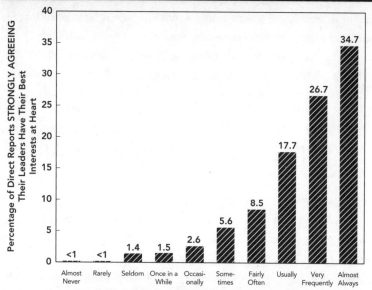

Figure 5.1 The more frequently people are afforded opportunities to grow and develop themselves, the more they believe that leaders have their best interests at heart.

paradoxically, where it is safe to fail. In other words, when you are *learning* to do something you haven't done before, you're unlikely to get it right the first time—and maybe even the second or third. You have to feel safe to fail to persist in learning. Feeling safe comes from trusting the system and the people involved. This leads to a degree of comfort (safety), which produces an openness to consuming new information and developing new skills. When you don't feel safe, you are generally reluctant to make yourself vulnerable to accepting information about yourself and your capabilities that might seem threatening. The typical reactions are defensiveness, screening out criticism, and putting any blame on anyone or everyone else.

A learning climate is characterized by trust and openness, which bring a greater willingness to communicate about feelings and problems. People feel comfortable sharing concerns and mistakes without fear of embarrassment or retribution. As they are listened to and more information becomes available, they experience greater common ground and reasons to engage in cooperative behavior. People are less motivated to defend either themselves or the status quo. They know they can ask questions when they are unsure about something. Our data shows that the more frequently leaders are seen by their direct reports as asking, "What can we learn when things do not go as expected," the more highly they rate the effectiveness of their leaders. In addition, the more "personally" effective people feel in their jobs.

Self-Esteem is a Win for All

As one way to encourage the heart, the Pygmalion effect gets high ratings with exemplary leaders. In its simplest form, it boosts self-esteem. To speak metaphorically, it seeks and finds the beauty hidden in the stone. In fact, you might view increased self-esteem, produced by high expectations, as the fulcrum for leveraging change. Research and everyday experience confirm that people with high self-esteem, regardless of their age, level of education, or socioeconomic status, "feel unique, competent, secure, empowered, and connected to the people around them."[12]

To illustrate the power of self-esteem and self-fulfilling prophecies, social psychologists conducted a fascinating experiment.[13] They created a simulated organization and then recruited working professionals to manage it. These professionals were asked to match employee attributes with job requirements and master a complex set of decision-making rules for guiding and motivating their employees.

Half the professionals participating in this experiment were told that decision-making skills are developed through practice—that is, they are *acquired* skills. The other half were told that such skills reflect one's essential cognitive capacities, meaning they are *stable* skills. Thus, one group worked from the premise that decision-making could be learned (a growth mindset); the other worked from the premise that you either have these skills or you don't (a fixed mindset).

The two professional groups were then given management tasks that included motivating people participating in the simulation as employees. Throughout the simulation, the subjects were asked to rate their effectiveness in getting the group they managed to perform at the desired productivity levels. Initially, both managerial groups expressed a moderately strong sense of organizational effectiveness. However, the stable-skill group's self-ratings plummeted as they tried to get their employees to fulfill increasingly difficult production standards. Similarly, as their self-perceptions fell, their attitudes toward their employees became quite uncharitable; they began regarding their subordinates as incapable of being motivated, unworthy of supervision, and deserving of termination.

Those managers in the acquired-skill group, who were having exactly the same problems as the stable-skilled group, maintained a high level of perceived self-efficacy. Since they believed their abilities could be acquired, they set more challenging goals and used analytical strategies excellently. They believed they could learn, so they did. This conviction influenced their belief in and behavior toward others.

Antonio Zarate demonstrated the power of this principle in real life. He led the turnaround of an automotive metal stamping company outside of Monterrey, Mexico, from one with a 10 percent rejection rate and only a domestic market into an award-winning, world-class business with 40 percent exports. He accomplished all this with the same local workforce who staffed the company when he took on the challenge. The difference was that Antonio believed the workers could do it. He pinpointed the most frequent reasons for product rejection and allocated resources to train employees in those areas. Most importantly, Antonio worked hard to demonstrate to his team that he believed they could be a world-class business, taking opportunities to reinforce this in both team and individual meetings. He believed that there were no poor-quality workers, only *under-led employees*. He never gave up on his workers—and he never gave up on himself.

We learn from all this that you must believe in others and yourself before you can encourage the heart. Your belief in others has positive benefits for individual leaders, their constituents, and the organizations they serve. High expectations matter—a lot.

The thoughts and beliefs you hold in your mind are intangible. They can't be weighed and measured like raw materials and the finished products that run off the assembly line. But seen or not, measurable or not, they impact the people around you enormously. Exemplary leaders know this and know how to purposefully hold high expectations for themselves and others in their heads and hearts.

With the attitude that people live up to high expectations and with clear standards, leaders have to pay attention to what's happening around them so they can find positive examples to recognize. In the next chapter, we will examine what it means to *pay attention* to what's happening around you.

REFLECT ON
EXPECTING THE BEST

Ask Yourself:

1. How high are my expectations for myself and others?
2. How effectively am I communicating these expectations?
3. How do my expectations result in behaviors contributing to low performance? To high performance?
4. What images of the future do I have in my mind right now? Are they primarily positive or mostly negative?
5. How am I communicating these images of the future right now? What else should I be doing?
6. How can I find even more opportunities to build the competence and confidence of the people I work with?
7. How can I strengthen my mindset that people can grow and develop themselves?

CHAPTER 6

The Third Essential

Pay Attention

Creative leaders find ways of stepping into the shoes of other people and asking, "How would I feel and what would I want if I were this person?"
—GAY HENDRICKS and KATE LUDEMAN
The Corporate Mystic: A Guidebook for Visionaries with
Their Feet on the Ground

IF YOU ARE clear about the standards of behavior you're looking for, and you believe and expect that people will perform like winners, you'll be much more inclined to pay attention to what's happening around you. That means paying attention to and noticing how well people are doing or not. But it's one thing to be able to do this when everyone is in the same location daily, and it's different when people work from home and in remote locations.

With the outbreak of the COVID-19 pandemic, Sean McLaughlin, vice president of news content for a national media company, realized he had to radically change the frequency, format, content, and purpose of calls with his nationwide team of news directors. The old routine of a once-a-year in-person meeting and twice-a-year conference calls could not possibly be enough to enable team members to do their best work, so Sean started checking in with everyone twice a week through video calling. The impact on Sean and the team was powerful.

Because the calls came from his home, they took on a more casual and personal tone. As Sean reflected, "We shared a lot more than before. Everyone was just more comfortable." Additionally, because he *saw* team members on video, he could more clearly observe when someone was fatigued and sense any feelings of anxiety or burnout. "Many times, I saw people who looked as if they were simply beat up and needed help," Sean said. "I would immediately turn around and reach out to them. I had never done that before."

Sean experienced firsthand how important it was to pay attention, actively listen, and be in tune with the emotional states of others, and he was reminded of how much the little things matter. "I would frequently tell people, 'Thank you, I am here for you, I understand how you are feeling.' I could see the relief in them." Sean summed it up this way: "You really do need to know how people are doing." This means you need to intentionally look for signs of how people feel and reach out whenever you notice that people might be experiencing difficulties or have achieved a significant milestone. Our research shows that nearly nine out of ten direct reports agree that when their leader almost always listens, they describe themselves as having a "strong sense of team spirit." When leaders are seen as not paying attention, less than one in fifty reports experiencing intense levels of team spirit.

Paying attention is a critical signal that you care about people, their actions, and how they feel. It's also about being curious enough to be "out and about," whether physically or virtually, to look around, ask questions, and listen. It becomes an ingrained habit for exemplary leaders to wander; it goes with the territory. In fact, at its root, the word *lead* comes from an Old English word that means "to go, travel, guide." The point is that wherever you are you must pay attention to the people you lead and intentionally search for ways to support and recognize them.

Release the Positive

What happens in organizations where managers are constantly looking for problems? Three things. First, they get a distorted view of reality. Second, over time, production declines. Third, the manager's personal credibility sinks to the bottom.

Put yourself in the employees' shoes. How would you behave if you knew someone was coming around to check up on you? You may think you are on your best behavior when you spot the boss coming, but this is not necessarily true. You may behave differently, but it's seldom your *best*. It can even be your worst. Why? Because you get nervous and tense, and you make more mistakes when you feel this way. The manager who wanders around with an eye out for trouble is likelier to get more trouble.

Controlling managers also have low credibility. Their behaviors—inspecting, correcting, checking up, watching over, wanting to see work before it goes out—signal that they don't trust you. How do you respond to someone who doesn't trust you? You don't trust them. And since trustworthiness is a critical element of personal credibility, credibility is diminished.[1]

So the first thing you've got to do when walking around your organization is to ditch the inspector's magnifying glass. Instead, put on your Pygmalion glasses and expect to find the best. If you see yourself as a caring leader, you act differently than when you see yourself as a controller. You express joy in seeing others succeed, you cheer others along, and you offer supportive coaching rather than being an authority figure who is out patrolling the neighborhood.

As you take on the caring leader role, people relate to you differently. They get the message that you're not out looking for ways to catch them screwing up but are instead looking for the opposite. In this environment, people open up. They no longer dread seeing you coming down the aisle or waiting for your image to appear on their screen while on a video call.

If people know there's a caring leader in their midst who actively seeks out achievements to celebrate, it naturally motivates them to show you something you can honor and celebrate. They relax and want to offer the best of themselves. This positive focus on behavior and performance, linked to goals and values, significantly improves morale as it moves the company toward higher levels of performance and increased productivity.

This was David Condon's experience when he moved into a senior product development manager position and was, as he put it, "feeling the pressure to get it right." He described himself as the type of person who, at the end of the day, trusted himself to get the job done. And David felt that if he wasn't involved in every aspect of a project, he couldn't be sure it would turn out okay. However, he soon found himself overwhelmed. More importantly, he noticed that checking in with everyone fairly often about how their work was going and what approaches they were taking— "Had they tried this or that?"—made people question their own judgment and wonder if they were doing a good job. They were worried that they weren't meeting David's expectations, which, according to David, wasn't true. He took a step back and said to himself:

> This is a great team. They don't always do things as I would, but they don't have to. I realized that my constant check-ins felt judgmental, and it was creating an atmosphere where people didn't feel trusted or respected. I decided to try something more positive. I ensured we were all on the same page about timelines and deliverables, and then stepped back and let people work, knowing that I cared about them and believed in their ability to succeed.

David admitted that this was initially hard for him, but he could literally feel his team relax. He realized that giving them the room to breathe and do their work their way was not just about autonomy; it also demonstrated how he trusted his team and showed he cared about their experience. The lesson learned for him, he explained, was that "when you show you care about people, I think they take on for themselves the responsibility to continue doing great work in unique and innovative ways."

In a supportive climate, David also noticed that people are likelier to help each other succeed. They teach and coach each other—another boost to productivity. In addition, in this open environment, people are more likely to let you know when problems are brewing and lend a hand in solving them before they escalate.

When we asked Renee Pearce, senior vice president with a global semiconductor company, to describe her personal-best leadership experience, she told us how she went to great lengths to acknowledge the contributions of people, both within and outside her organization: "I would see great things that were going on in marketing, for example, and I'd tell them, 'Way to go!' I'd hear about a new initiative in product development, and I'd go into the lab and tell them, 'Fantastic!' If they figured out a more efficient sales reporting process in the field, I'd reach out and find those responsible and let them know how much we appreciated their initiative." That's what caring leaders do, and that's one of the reasons why, for Renee, such actions resulted in a personal best.

Know Your Audience

Much like David and Renee demonstrated, paying attention lets you know your audience, who your people and colleagues are, what they care about, and how to understand what motivates each person individually. For some, it may be a simple thank you; others may require a much grander gesture, such as acknowledgment in a public forum or prominently displaying their name online. Regardless of the way someone is celebrated, it must be sincere.

Kim White told us about one of her key takeaways from the pandemic: how previously unnoticed employees were now being recognized. Before the pandemic, recognition for the contributions of her facilities team was often overlooked. Their job was to ensure everyone was safe, the building was up to code, and supplies were stocked at adequate levels. However, what "safe" looked like changed when the pandemic hit, and ordering supplies became much more complicated and complex. They now had to become creative and work even harder with their suppliers to obtain, for example, toilet paper and cleaning supplies. The team worked around the clock to ensure all the right signs were posted at each location and employees felt safe in the building. Others around the organization could now see how critical the facilities team was to the company and their daily lives at work. "We were able," Kim said, "to acknowledge and celebrate this team on a public platform in front of the entire organization—something that had not been done since they began their tenure fifteen years ago."

Leaders sometimes have to learn what their audience needs the hard way, as Wendy Monteverdi's experience illustrates. Unexpectedly, a very valuable member of her team (Brittney) submitted her resignation along with a very impassioned letter. Brittney felt overworked, underappreciated, and unmotivated; she couldn't see past what was before her, and she struggled to get through every day. Wendy was devastated:

> Brittney was the strongest person on my team, and I let her burn out. How could I have let this happen? I had such high hopes for her journey with us; how could I let her give up? I hired her, trained her, promised her the world, and then failed her. I felt the heavy weight of failure crushing my chest as I sat silently for a couple of hours after receiving her letter.

Wendy finally called her. Texted her. Emailed her. No response. Ghosted. The CEO called Wendy because he knew how much Brittney meant to the firm. His words to Wendy were straightforward: "I know you can turn this around. I believe in you." This message of confidence lifted Wendy's spirits, and she continued to reach out until Brittney was ready to talk.

Wendy asked Brittney to paint a picture of what she wanted for herself—in her dream job, what she was doing, and what kind of environment she was working in. After Brittney shared this, Wendy asked her if she would consider staying if she could provide her with the environment she was looking for and the opportunity to grow into whatever position she wished. Wendy shared with Brittney all the reasons why she hired her in the first place, reiterating the value she added to the company and how she saw her fitting into the firm's overall vision. In response, Wendy saw "the joy in her eyes come back, and felt her excitement ramp up." She brought Brittney back on board, gave her a promotion, made the announcement public, and assigned her several mission-critical projects that were also meaningful to her personal and professional growth objectives. In relating this experience with us, Wendy realized:

> This leadership practice is probably one that I've taken for granted until the moment Brittney quit. I realized that encouraging the heart meant I had to humble my heart first. I had to put myself in a position of empathy. It forced me to listen, endure the pain of failure, and experience what it was like to have my own heart encouraged by my CEO. Only then did I find clarity around what it would take to encourage Brittney's heart; thankfully, it wasn't too late.

Leaders realize that they must know their audience, whether it's one individual (as in Wendy's situation) or the entire team (as in Kim's example). Paying attention demonstrates your interest and confidence in what people can do and how you trust them to use their best judgment. It can be all too easy to take your constituents' work for granted and categorize it as "just part of their job." The experiences of Kim, Wendy, and scores of others demonstrate the importance of acknowledging and recognizing people meaningfully. To encourage others, you must focus on the positive. Doing so shows others that you're their biggest supporter and underscores how much you appreciate and value them.

Listen With Your Eyes and Your Heart

Central to knowing your audience is the capacity to walk in their shoes; understanding and seeing things from another's point of view is crucial to building trusting relations and attaining their success. For example, studies from the Center for Creative Leadership reveal that successful executives most often derailed because of insensitivity and inability to understand other people's perspectives. They undervalued the contributions of others, making them feel inadequate. They listened poorly, acted dictatorially, played favorites, and failed to give—or sometimes even share—credit with others. The net result over time was that these traits and attitudes caught up with them. When these managers really needed the help of others around them, they were left to fend for themselves, ignored, isolated, and, on occasion, purposely sabotaged.[3]

Listening is a crucial leadership skill. But not just any kind of listening.

We attended the annual fundraising breakfast for an extraordinary nonprofit job training and placement organization a while back. One of the speakers was Michael Pritchard, a youth counselor and probation officer by day and a standup comic by night. He told a story that morning that we'll never forget.

Michael was visiting an elementary school and got to talking with a third grader. He asked her what she'd been learning, and she said sign language. Michael was intrigued by her response. Sign language? Kids don't typically learn sign language in third grade. So he asked how she got started on that educational adventure.

The young girl explained that her best friend from first grade couldn't speak or hear. She asked her mom if she could learn sign language to communicate with her friend. Her mom said yes and began to drive her daughter back and forth to lessons.

"Now," the young girl said, "I listen with my eyes and with my heart, not just my ears and my brain." Wow! What a lesson that is.

All leaders can learn from this third grader. Listening with your eyes and hearts, not just your ears and brains, requires a deeper level of paying attention. It requires that you listen for understanding and not only for the words; you hear the heart and see the soul. It's the only kind of listening that genuinely creates a capacity to encourage the heart.

There's another lesson from this story. The young girl's mom listened, *paid attention* to her daughter's needs, and helped her learn sign language. Imagine how this would have turned out if her mom had not paid attention and not supported her daughter's request. Listening and paying attention have benefits that extend well beyond the initial encounter.

Scholars have pointed out that in listening, it's "not the content of the exchange that is central but the experience of being taken in and heard, which not only affirms the legitimacy of one's way of looking at the world but then allows one to begin letting go of some defensiveness because the experience of affirmation increases one's capacity to affirm others."[5] Academy Award–winning actress Annette Bening's experience supports the findings in this research. You may think you are most present for others when talking, but Annette says we're more authentically "there" when we listen. "As a parent," she says, "one of the things I'm trying hardest to do is to listen. Our instinct as parents is to talk: 'I'm worried about you, I have all this experience and wisdom, and I want to tell you about what you need to know.'" But to listen, she maintains, is to move over and truly make room for another person, understanding who they are and allowing this experience to help shape who we are in respect to them.[6]

Bill Curtis admits that he talks too much, which he explains is because "I get so excited by the work that it causes my brain to spin faster and start trying to execute before others are comfortable with it." He realized that to be a better leader, he needed to be a better listener. He found that not interrupting people with whom he interacted had an immediate and noticeable effect, improving his relationships with colleagues:

> There are elements in conversations I used to miss that I am now picking up on. One of my managers even remarked on this behavior, noting that I had shifted from "leading by telling" to "leading by asking." This difference has led to a palpable response to my leadership. I don't believe that I changed the content of my messaging, but others now listen more closely to what I have to say, all because I now deliberately listen to what they say. The team feels heard and recognized.

As basic as this might seem, listening is not all that universal. More than twenty years ago, research by the Hay Group, covering one million employees in more than two thousand organizations, revealed that only about one in three people respond favorably to questions about how well their company listens to them.[7] A recent study still finds that more than one-third of employees don't believe their company listens to their ideas.[8] Another survey reports that nearly nine in ten employees don't feel people at their organization are heard fairly or equally. Of those, nearly half indicate that employees identifying as underserved races and ethnicities and younger workers are undervalued by their employers.[9]

Eyes-and-heart listening can't be conducted from a distance by reading reports or hearing things secondhand. The people you work with want to know who you are, how you feel, and whether you care. They want to see you in living color. You must get close if you're going to listen. You often have to visit them because most constituents cannot come to you. This means regularly walking the office hallways and plant floors, visiting the labs, meeting with small groups in person or virtually, and hitting the road for frequent visits with associates, key suppliers, and customers. It means getting on the phone when you feel someone needs your support or scheduling a video conference simply because you haven't heard from someone in a while. It may even mean learning another language if a portion of your workforce or customer base speaks it.

What's so amazing about the third-grader's story is that she learned the language of another to strengthen their relationship. You might say, "Well, that's because she had to if she wanted to be her friend." Precisely! She had to learn sign language if she wanted to be a friend. Learning another's language, literally or figuratively, is essential to caring leadership. Only by discovering what others value, what they enjoy and treasure, can you expect to reach their hearts.

Who do you trust more, someone you know or don't know? Whenever we ask people this question, the universal answer is, "Someone I know." Of course, there may be people you know you don't trust at all, but generally, people are much more likely to trust friends than strangers. When paying attention to the positive, you're highly visible and make yourself known to others. While you're getting to know them, they're getting to know you. A side benefit of actively paying attention to and appreciating others is that their trust in you increases. This kind of relationship is more critical than ever as the workforce becomes more global, diverse, and virtual. If others know you genuinely care about them, they're more likely to care about you. This is how you bridge cultural divides.

Hang Out

Gretchen Kaffer, a human resource professional, learned the value of listening and being physically present when her department reorganized. She used to spend time in the cafeteria and on the patio chatting with her coworkers during lunch hour, but she'd gotten too busy. With the reorganization, Gretchen's group moved into a refurbished building with a spacious new break room where four to five people could gather comfortably. She noticed that since the move, people began to hang out in the break room for lunch. Gretchen decided she needed to get out of her office more and made joining her colleagues at lunch a regularly scheduled part of her day.

"The first couple of times I popped in," she reports, "everyone looked up at me as if I was coming to ask someone a work-related question. They were surprised that I was joining them for lunch. Some people may have thought I didn't want to spend time with them because I hadn't done so in a while."

Gretchen likes to know what's going on with her coworkers. She likes "to be sensitive and approach people in a manner in which I think they'll be most receptive," but her absence created some distance. It didn't take long before Gretchen started to learn all sorts of things about her colleagues that she'd missed.

She told us it also opened up good conversations about work and nonwork-related issues and events. It allowed her and her colleagues to "hash over" some changes and procedures that they wouldn't usually get to discuss in their large division meetings. Just hanging out at lunch or connecting informally over cell phone or video calls allows people to ask questions, make suggestions, and offer various perspectives. Gretchen learned considerably more about what was happening now that she was "no longer cooped up in my office." There was another benefit to the "lunch club thing," as they called it. Gretchen recounted:

> Employees from other departments seem pleasantly surprised by the laughter from our break room. They walk by and sometimes stop and ask if we are having a party. We often invite them to join us. I think this has definitely improved our image as a team, given us greater visibility, and allowed us to interact more with other employees in our building.

Whether it's joining the lunch club or walking the plant floor, hosting video chats, or putting your cell phone on speaker and sitting back and chatting, being present and paying attention to the concerns and accomplishments of others allows leaders to gather critical information. Some of this information is valuable in solving problems, and some in recognizing contributions. The message from Gretchen is that you've got to be there to gather it. Funny thing: when you begin to hang out with folks, and they know you're interested in them, they *want* to see you. Other people notice as well, and they want to join in, too. People like to be where and with people who are enjoying themselves.

Be a Friend and Open Up

You may have been told that it's dangerous to get too close to your constituents or be friends with people at work. Well, set this myth aside.

Over a five-year period, researchers observed groups of friends and groups of acquaintances (that is, people who knew each other only vaguely) while performing motor skill and decision-making tasks in two different situations. On one, they built models out of Tinker Toys. On the other, they ranked actual MBA candidates against a specified criteria. Both groups' decisions were compared to those of the actual admissions committee. The results were unequivocal, with friends completing an average of nine Tinker Toy models compared with the acquaintances' average of 2.45. In the decision-making situation, friends accurately matched an average of 3.1 of five possible admissions committee decisions, whereas acquaintances averaged 2.4 matches.[10] Gallup surveys continue to show that having a best friend at work is strongly linked to improvements in profitability, job satisfaction, and retention, even considering the rise of remote and hybrid work.[11]

A critical caveat to interpreting these results is that a group of friends has to be strongly committed to the group's goals, otherwise they may not do better than acquaintances. This is precisely why we said earlier that leaders must be clear about standards and create a condition of shared goals and values. Regarding performance, commitment to standards and good relationships between people go together.

There's also strong evidence that people listen more intently when they perceive the speaker as a friend—someone with their best interests in mind—than someone they perceive only as a professional associate. Friends and family are always the most important sources for information about healthcare, restaurants, where to go on a vacation, or what kind of new car to buy. Similarly, leaders who get out there and let themselves be known are much more likely to be accepted as "family" members than those who don't.

People are more willing to follow someone they like and trust. To become fully trusted, you must be open to and *with* others. An open door is a physical demonstration of a willingness to let others in. So is an open heart. This means disclosing things about yourself. We don't mean the tabloid-like disclosures that seem to haunt leaders today. We suggest openly discussing your hopes and dreams, family and friends, interests, and pursuits. We encourage you to tell others the same things you'd like to know about them.

When you are open, you make yourself vulnerable. But this vulnerability makes you more human and, correspondingly, more trusted. If neither person in a relationship takes the risk of trusting, at least a little, the relationship remains stalled at a low level of caution and suspicion.

If leaders want the higher levels of performance that come with trust and collaboration, they must demonstrate their trust *in* others before asking for trust *from* others. When it comes to trust, leaders ante up first.

We get it. Disclosing information about yourself can be risky.[12] You can't be sure that other people will like you, appreciate your honesty, agree with your aspirations, buy into your plans, or interpret your words and actions as you intend. However, leaders encourage others to reciprocate by demonstrating a willingness to take such risks. Once the leader takes the risk of being open, others are more likely to take a similar risk, thereby taking the first steps necessary to building interpersonal trust.

Disclosing information about yourself is one way to be open. Asking for constructive feedback is another—not merely giving feedback to others but asking for it yourself. When you're out there attending to what's happening and noticing people's positive contributions, stop and ask them for feedback. It's a demonstration that you appreciate them. By being open to influence, leaders encourage people to provide more information.[13]

"How am I doing?" might not initially seem like something a leader would ask, but it is a practice of the best leaders. Soliciting feedback is the reciprocal side of showing appreciation. Recognizing another's contribution is your gift to others, and feedback is their gift to you. It's a gift of information that enables you to grow and improve.

Seek and Ye Shall Find

When you seriously pay attention—when you're curious, looking for the best, putting others first, listening with eyes and heart, hanging out, and opening up to and with others—then you find what you seek. You notice all kinds of examples of people living up to and exceeding the standards that have been set. You find lots of opportunities to recognize individuals for their contributions.

REFLECT ON
PAYING ATTENTION

Ask Yourself:

1. How often am I demonstrating caring by wandering around?
2. What do I notice more often—what's working or what's wrong?
3. How well do people know me? What have I shared about my hopes, dreams, joys, passions, life, and so on? Where are opportunities to share more about myself?
4. What do I know about the needs, hopes, and dreams of those I work with?
5. What can I do so that people would say I am a good listener?
6. Where can I "hang out" more often?
7. Who do I open up to at work, and who are others with whom I can be more open? Who would I say are my "friends" at work?

CHAPTER 7

The Fourth Essential

Personalize Recognition

Recognize teammates' individual psychology and the best ways to motivate them. Great leaders recognize these things instinctively and are able to find each person's motivational levers.

—*TOM BRADY*
Entrepreneur and Former NFL (GOAT) Quarterback

SHORTLY AFTER ONE of his workshops, Steve Farber received a thank-you note from one of the participants. Steve is a highly accomplished trainer and presenter who gets lots of thank-you notes. But this one was special.

It was sent to Steve but addressed to his son.

Here's the letter verbatim:

Steve's Son,

I understand you're curious about what your dad does when his job takes him away from home. I'll bet it's tough on you sometimes to have him away when you'd like to have him home more than he is. As one of his students this past week,

I thought you might want to know what he did to help me and others in the class that he taught.

Your dad has valuable knowledge about how businesses work and how to improve them. Even more importantly, he helps people make their lives better and happier. He teaches all this in a fun way, so the time we spend with him in class is really enjoyable.

I just wanted you to know that we very much appreciated your sharing him this week. If he's anywhere near as good or as fun as a father as he is as a teacher, you've got yourself one fine dad.

Carl English

One of your dad's students

This simple thank-you note is an extraordinary example of how someone can turn something commonplace into a unique event. Carl, vice president of a utility company, *personalized* his recognition. He could have purchased a preprinted thank-you card and then written a perfunctory note inside about how much he enjoyed being in the class. But he didn't.

Carl understood the importance of paying attention. He took the time to learn that Steve had a son who was curious about what his dad did at work. He wrote the note to the son, praising his dad for an exemplary job. This extra effort made the note something Steve treasures and loves sharing with others. Steve told us, "That note made a huge difference. As much as I love my work—and I do—on those days when I'd rather be at home with my family than out on the road somewhere, I think of that note, and it reminds me why I go to work every day."

Nobody expressed surprise when Steve shared this note in subsequent workshops with the utility company. Carl was known for the personal notes he wrote to people. If you really care about others, you pay attention to them. You find something unique to say. Even if Carl's writing his one hundredth or one thousandth note, he takes the time and effort to make it unique because he knows his colleagues and how to provide a meaningful message.

Similarly, Donna Rogers described her reaction to a "standard email from the leadership team" congratulating all those involved in securing a major contract to provide sales engineering support to several strategic cloud accounts. She immediately saw the problem: no real acknowledgment was directed to each person who had worked so diligently to produce the winning proposal. This was a generic "great job, everyone" email sent to a distribution of more than fifty people, many of them only indirectly involved. Donna took it upon herself to take several steps to make this right:

> First, I identified each and every person who made a significant contribution to the project—the thirty core contributors. Second, in a short yet comprehensive summary, I noted precisely what they did and how it contributed to the winning proposal. I sent these to our senior leadership team and publicly acknowledged their contributions. In addition, I created a recognition award for each person involved. I worked with the different leadership teams across the sites to develop a meaningful gift tailored to their geographies.

So who says business isn't personal? It *is* personal, and you want to make it that way.

Personalization Matters

To truly recognize people so they are encouraged by your efforts, you must know something about who they are—some of their likes and dislikes, whether they enjoy public recognition or shirk from it, and even what they are or are not willing to take credit for. We pointed this out in the last chapter. Failing to pay attention and learning something about others can result in an act of recognition without meaning. In fact, it can even hurt.

Rebecca Morgan is an author, speaker, and managing partner of her consulting firm on the West Coast. She told us a poignant story about a time when a well-meaning act of recognition boomeranged. It's an example of what *not* to do.

Rebecca is a person who likes recognition that is "either one-to-one with me or in front of a group that is significant to me, that is sincere, shows appreciation, and is directed to my specific contributions and the effect they had on the project." Unfortunately, in the case she related to us, this did not happen. She tells it this way:

> The president of one of my professional associations once brought me and a handful of volunteers on stage at the end of a convention where I had served as logistics chair. I expected, perhaps, a few sentences about the two years I'd served on the committee preparing for the event, the two cross-country flights I'd made at my own expense for committee meetings, the hundreds of hours I'd put in, and the one hundred volunteers I'd recruited and trained.
>
> Instead, he said two sentences I'll never forget: "Rebecca did the little things. If no one else would do it, we knew Rebecca would." I was stunned, crushed. It sounded like I'd collated a few packages or made some copies. I could barely see my sixteen hundred colleagues giving us a standing ovation. When I got off stage, I had to leave the room. I cried for an hour. He meant well; he just hadn't thought much about what he would say until we were on stage. Now, I know that when I acknowledge someone, I need to be clear on how to phrase this to leave the person feeling honored, not diminished.

Honored and not diminished—that's how everyone wants to feel. You can only genuinely honor someone when you know who they are, what they like, and what they've done. You have to have the person in mind. For instance, Carl thought, "I want to honor our seminar leader. How can I make this special for him?" For the company president, the thought should have been: "I want to honor Rebecca; what can I say and do to make this special for her?"

Jackalyn Hurdle clearly understood that recognition and appreciation are most meaningful when they are authentic and sincere. Moreover, recognition and appreciation mean even more when they come unexpectedly from someone important for something they are proud of. She shared with us a project where she experienced how important these are to encouraging the heart. After the conclusion of a major vendor exposition that she helped organize, the agent of one of the keynote artists contacted her out of the blue. The agent wanted to let her know the artist had a really wonderful time and wanted to thank her personally. Later that year, Jackalyn was invited to a celebratory thank-you lunch in Japan by the artist and agent to recognize the work she had done for them. They solidified their relationship so that Jackalyn could contract with the artist for future collaborations. "Having experienced this," Jackalyn told us:

> I have taken the same approach with teams that I've worked with, where I try to show my appreciation for their work. I also provide small gestures to arouse their internal drive to be their best and find ways to celebrate our wins to ensure that people continue to feel like they are part of my networked community.

Anne Cessaris has an international set of consulting clients, and she reminds us of another reason why it's essential to personalize, or should we say, "culturalize" recognition. "I had a client," she reported, "born in Asia, came to this country at age twelve, and was very well acclimated to life in the United States. However, when his boss rewarded his exceptional contribution to a team project by giving him a delightful corner office, he was horrified. He felt it destroyed the feeling of teamwork and his future relations with his team members."

As these examples illustrate, you must communicate you know the people you work with. Personalized recognition leaves a lasting imprint and is ultimately the kind of acknowledgment that makes a difference to people. It holds far more value than some bonus on a paycheck or generic gift certificate that quickly fades from memory.[1] Personalizing is about knowing the other so well that you know what's appropriate, not just individually but culturally. It's fairly arrogant for anyone, let alone because they are in a management position, to assume they naturally know what's suitable for others without even bothering to inquire or observe.

Know What they Like

David Bonilla, president of a business advisory firm, told us another story that drives home the point about *knowing*. His wife left her job as an administrative secretary for a more meaningful position with a local church. At a Sunday morning worship, the staff recognized her seventeen-year service to the group by presenting her with a silver jewelry dish. Although the gift was generous in one respect, it fell far short of the goal of giving meaningful recognition because nobody asked David or his wife what she might like. It just so happened that she had never liked silver!

"Instead of being impressed or feeling appreciated," David told us, "she felt more ignored, discouraged, and resentful. So the moral of this story," he went on, "reinforces an old concept I heard somewhere. A manager should ask employees how they would like to be recognized. Different motivations drive all of us—some slightly different, some greatly different."

While researching this book, David's story sparked a vigorous debate in our online chat group where people exchanged ideas with us on this subject. Most thought asking before giving was appropriate, but others thought it spoiled the surprise and detracted from the primary intent.

We'll let you decide on this issue, but David's sentiments seem sound. If you don't know what people like to receive, it's better to ask them than to risk creating resentment for an otherwise well-intentioned gesture. A caring leader can learn a person's likes and dislikes from friends, coworkers, and family members, and direct observation. Most of their time, asking the recipient directly should never be necessary. After all, don't you explore what your family members want to receive when you're getting ready for a special occasion? What's getting in the way of doing that with colleagues at work?

Sridhar Alsaddiki was having lunch one day with his manager, and the conversation gravitated toward an upcoming complex and challenging work assignment. He got excited about the project and volunteered to take it on, and Sridhar recalls: "Fortunately, it turned out to be a success." He told us how pleasantly surprised he was a few weeks after the project was completed to receive a personalized gift from his manager. It was a Civil War book series, which Sridhar described as "a thoughtful gesture" due to his passion for American history. "This act of personalized recognition," Sridhar told us, "meant more to me than just a gift. It made me feel valued and genuinely appreciated."

There are at least three reasons why notes of appreciation are so impactful.[2] For one, they help people see their own strengths, minimizing the likelihood of them feeling undervalued or dismissed because those strengths come naturally. Second, they focus the recipient's attention on what's working, at least from someone else's perspective, which tends to reinforce the behaviors and actions noticed. Third, they are a visible reminder and signal that the recipient matters and their actions make a difference.

Be Creative

People respond to all kinds of recognition and rewards other than promotions and raises. Research suggests that informal awards—such as congratulatory cards, public recognition, and certificates—can significantly increase intrinsic motivation, performance, and retention rates. In one study, workers who received personalized letters of appreciation sent to their home addresses from their direct managers reported feeling significantly more valued and supported by their organization than those who did not receive the letter.[3]

Tom Atwell is a shop foreman who presents employees who achieve their production objectives with a new chair for the workplace. The chairs alone are a good reward, but a major part of the reward—the part that's even more pleasurable than comfortable seating for the employees—comes with the presentation. The rewarded employee is called into Tom's office and presented with the new chair. Tom then wheels that individual in the chair back to their workstation—amid the whoops and hollers of coworkers.

Here are some other possibilities: photographs with senior executives, verbal encouragement, spot awards, pictures in annual reports, stories in company newsletters, blog postings, publishing thank-you notes, contributions to employees' favorite charities, gift certificates and merchandise credits, gifts for families and partners, banners displayed in the cafeteria, and symbolic stuffed animals, to name a few. Kendall Finch, a university colleague, takes his highest-performing students each term for lunch and bowling to show his appreciation for their hard work. In a virtual environment, you could throw a party over Zoom, organize a virtual scavenger hunt, or create a personalized thank-you video from colleagues worldwide to celebrate individual achievements. There's no limit—except your imagination—to creative recognition.

Maureen Mitchell wondered how to show her appreciation to her family for all the ways they stepped up and dealt with several loved ones with life-threatening illnesses during the pandemic. She decided to think outside the box and gathered everyone on Zoom for an Awards Ceremony. Everyone received an award and meaningful title for something positive they had done. Her older sister, Jeanie, was awarded for her courageousness as the CEO of the family. Cousin Lily was dubbed Vice President of Internal Affairs for caring for anything needed at home. The title of Vice President of Technology went to Lynn, another cousin, for all his work keeping everyone connected virtually and problem-solving the many computer glitches that inevitably arose. Maureen's brother KJ was crowned Vice President of Logistics and was awarded for his outstanding attention to detail when coordinating the master family calendar. Her other brother Gary was named Vice President of Transportation since he was one of the main drivers to all the appointments. This whimsical celebration made everyone smile—something that lifted their spirits and made them appreciate one another and being part of this family.

If you need help being creative, discuss the possibilities with your team members. Ask them what they find encouraging and consider their ideas about how they would go about encouraging others. For example, what types of encouragement make the difference for you? What stood out whenever you've felt encouraged, supported, or cared about? What comes to mind about the best recognition experience you've ever had? You can also think about some of the talents on your team that could be used to recognize and encourage others. All in all, discuss what you and your teammates could do to support one another better. Remember that a large part of the pleasure in giving and receiving recognition comes from its sincerity and personalization.

While we're on this subject of creativity, you might wonder where cash as recognition and a reward comes in. Researchers have found that cash awards are not very memorable. Almost one in every five employees will not even remember where they spent the money. The number one use of cash awards is to pay bills.[4] Do you remember the amount of your last cash bonus? Do you remember what bills, credit cards, loans, or debts you paid off? If you did buy something for yourself (or your family), isn't that the thing you remember and not the cash amount? On the other hand, you can probably list every award you ever won in high school or college, even if it has been ten, twenty, thirty, or more years since.

An effective recognition event or celebration doesn't mean holding an elaborate banquet, shutting down the office or call center, closing the bank, or other costly events. It does, however, require that you take time to prepare in advance. Consider who should be in attendance given the purpose and people being recognized. If there's a presentation, choose the right person to make it, which doesn't necessarily mean a high-ranking officer. Please select the individual who personally knows the recipient and their accomplishments and contributions to ensure sincerity and meaning. Make sure that whoever is presenting knows precisely what is being recognized and can speak about specific contributions that have made a difference.

Ensure the recipients' actions are linked and tied to company values. You can ask colleagues and coworkers, and even users like clients and customers when appropriate, to comment on the difference that the recipient's actions have made on them and their work or lives. This helps everyone to understand and better appreciate the action being recognized, how it's related to the organization's goals and vision, and how others can emulate it.

Furthermore, consider allowing the recipient to make a few comments. Not everyone will want to do this, but they should be asked and given the opportunity. This provides the recipient with the chance to thank others who have helped them and talk about their emotional commitment to the goals and the organization. By their example, they show others in the audience how aspirations may be achieved and reinforce the sense of common purpose. Remember to wrap up the ceremony by offering your sincere thank-you, not just to the recipient, but to everyone in the audience, and let them know that you're on the lookout for people doing things right, and you plan to catch them at it!

Catch People Doing Things Right

Many managers, too often, tend to focus on what's not working and what's wrong, assigning blame and even punishment instead of finding what's right, recognizing, and celebrating it. The leadership challenge is proactively searching for, identifying, and recognizing people doing "it" right. Positive reinforcement keeps people engaged.[5]

Recognition is most effective when it is distinctive and given in close proximity to the appropriate behavior. To provide such timely feedback, you must be out and about, physically or virtually, finding the behaviors you want to foster. One of the most important benefits of doing so is that you can personally observe people doing things right and then reward them on the spot or at your next team meeting or public gathering.

Consider implementing a system for collecting information about people doing the right things from constituents and customers. Add this question to your meeting agendas: "Who have you seen doing something special that helped our customers and our organization?"

Once you've selected people for recognition, be sure to tell them—and everyone else—why they've been chosen. To gain the maximum benefit, tell the story of why the person (or people) is being recognized and make it specific. Merely saying, "Hey, you did a great job in handling that customer's concern last week," may sound pleasant enough, but in practical terms, it is a fairly worthless remark. The problem is the person you are praising has no idea what they did that impressed you or how they made a difference. Give as much information as possible about why you're pleased and how the person's actions have affected the larger picture. Remember that stories describing valued actions are compelling ways to communicate what behaviors are expected and will be rewarded (more on this in the next chapter). Walk people through the actions that contributed to goal attainment and explain why these were consistent with shared values.

You might say something along these lines: "Rob was selected as the employee of the month because he called five different stores to locate an item that a customer requested but that we didn't have in stock. And because that store couldn't deliver the item until the next week, he picked it up on his way home from work so the customer could have it in time for an important event. That's the kind of behavior that makes our company so highly valued by our customers. Thank you, Rob. We present you with this award in appreciation for your commitment to the company's value of delighting every customer."

This kind of positive example can be particularly beneficial when trying to help people understand the right things to do to achieve a higher standard. It provides a behavioral map that people can store in their minds and rely on when a similar situation arises in the future.

To broaden the net for capturing opportunities for recognition, set up systems for people to be recognized by their constituents, whether they're coworkers or customers, and not just managers. Many organizations have systems for "spot awards" that recognize exemplary behavior or performance as it happens. On-the-spot awards are often small tokens of recognition and appreciation, such as a gift card for dining, shopping, or an event, but they don't have to be tangible awards. A verbal thank-you from a colleague whose work has been impacted positively by another's action reinforces a culture of encouragement. It's another way of saying "I see you" and "I appreciate you." They are reminders that people's contributions have been noticed and their efforts are not being taken for granted.

This encourages everyone in the organization to be on the lookout for good behaviors and to be mindful that others are also observing their actions. In one Midwest nursing home, staff are recognized with a pin that says, "Caught Caring." In an environment where patients can't necessarily say "thank you," the pins mean much to staff members as they announce that someone recognizes how much they care and contribute.

The research shows that very few people feel the organization values their work unless they hear it from their leader. As the data in Figure 7.1 dramatically illustrates, when direct reports only *sometimes or less frequently receive praise for a job well done, they are unlikely to feel that their organization values their work*. In contrast, when their leader *almost always* recognizes good work, they have a strong sense that what they are doing is appreciated and that it matters.

There's a flip side to catching people doing things right, and that's to be on the lookout for signs of fatigue and stress, especially when efforts are below par and unnecessary errors occur. When under duress, people are more prone to making mistakes, and people struggling to sustain their efforts and commitment will also need to know that you care about them and understand the pressures they are facing. Part of personalizing recognition is showing empathy for others' circumstances and willingness to listen and understand their concerns. It's essential to fostering their resilience. In difficult times, people turn to others for strength and support, and you must show that you care in the bad times as well as when things are going well. *Compassion* means "to suffer together," and letting others know you are aware of their struggles sends an encouraging message. Better yet, jumping in to help out says even more.

Figure 7.1 Praise for a job well done increases feeling that one's work is valued.

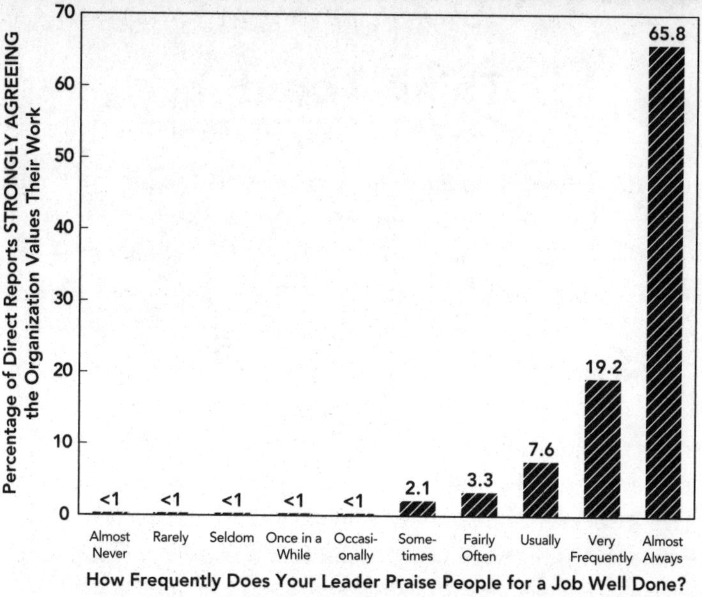

A bar chart. The vertical axis reads "Percentage of Direct Reports STRONGLY AGREEING the Organization Values Their Work" ranging from 0 to 70. The horizontal axis reads "How Frequently Does Your Leader Praise People for a Job Well Done?" with categories and values:

- Almost Never: <1
- Rarely: <1
- Seldom: <1
- Once in a While: <1
- Occasionally: <1
- Sometimes: 2.1
- Fairly Often: 3.3
- Usually: 7.6
- Very Frequently: 19.2
- Almost Always: 65.8

Troy Woodward, a regional manager with a financial services firm, knows leaders must be prepared to sacrifice and struggle alongside their people to overcome hardships and setbacks. About to leave for a long-delayed holiday, he couldn't help but notice that the team was generally complaining about the "unreasonable" demands from one of their largest clients, the "unreasonable" extra and unexpected work required, and the "unreasonable" time constraints. They harshly criticized others outside of the department for this circumstance, and he knew it would only be a matter of time before this snipping turned internal, pointing fingers and blaming their colleagues. Troy turned around, walked back in the door, dramatically rolled up his sleeves, and announced, "The beach can wait. Let's order some food and see what progress we can make in the next few hours and days to get this situation back on track. We've done it before, and we'll do it again this time," he said with a hearty smile. Troy's response and setting aside his needs energized the team and moved them from despair to making a difference.

Think About it

It boils down to *thoughtfulness*: how much effort you put into thinking about the other person and considering what will make the recognition memorable for them. It means observing an individual and asking: "What would make this special and unique for this person—make it a memorable, one-of-a-kind experience? How could I ensure they never forget how much they mean to us? What can I do to make sure they always remember how important their contributions are?" Researchers have found that employees were significantly more productive after receiving a physical, nonmonetary gift than when they received small financial gifts. Employees reported feeling more valued when they saw that their employer took the time and effort to choose, purchase, and wrap the gift. As a result, they increased their efforts in return.[6]

Such thoughtfulness was strikingly evident in this example of how Wayne Bennett recognized, celebrated, and showed appreciation for the efforts of one of his key employees. Wayne founded a unique startup company that builds computer-designed, precision-crafted custom homes in a small West Coast town.

Thanks to the early success of this startup, the new factory faced a backlog of home orders. Wayne needed a highly skilled production manager to meet the extraordinary challenge in front of them. From the pool of candidates, he selected Ray Freer, a veteran with fifteen years in the industry. He was an energetic worker whose talents and expertise had not been fully used in previous jobs. Ray was anxious for the opportunity to demonstrate his skills and abilities in setting up and running a factory, even though he was quite aware that the time and financial pressures were tremendous. Wayne believed in Ray and entrusted him with full responsibility to lead the crew.

Wayne's confidence in Ray was well-placed. They were ready to begin regular production after several six- and seven-day weeks. The plant was state-of-the-art, the previously inexperienced crew well-trained, and Ray had personally built and installed additional buffer stations to augment production during unexpected delays. The first house was successfully cut, sized, and shipped within three days of the start of production. Karen, one of Ray's coworkers, explained what was done to let Ray know that his efforts had made a difference:

> To acknowledge Ray's extraordinary accomplishment at the first president's barbecue, Wayne called the group to one side of the factory and asked Ray to demonstrate how one of the buffer stations worked. When Ray threw the lever to operate the skate-wheel conveyor, which he had personally designed and constructed, a spring-loaded rod was unexpectedly released, displaying a flag with an envelope attached. When Ray looked inside the envelope, he found a five-hundred-dollar check and a handwritten letter from Wayne thanking him for his outstanding work.
>
> Wayne then read the letter to the group, acknowledging the importance of Ray's creativity and hard work in preparing the production area in time to meet the first influx of home orders. Ray was clearly moved by Wayne's public display of appreciation. The vigorous clapping and loud cheers of Ray's coworkers and crew visibly demonstrated their mutual support for his well-earned award.

Wayne had obviously put some *thought* into this recognition. He closely observed what Ray had done to contribute to the success of the factory, and he actually used equipment that Ray had personally constructed as an integral part of the celebration. Wayne then read aloud a personal note he'd written Ray, telling of his innovativeness, dedication, and tireless work on behalf of the company. A check always helps, and the boss can always hand it to the employee in private without all the rest of the ceremony. But not Wayne. He knew that personalizing recognition and telling the story publicly would be more meaningful and reinforce a a sense of purpose for everyone involved.

You have to have a "method to your madness" when, like Wayne, you are being creative and personally involved in encouraging the heart. Alan Neiss, head of talent and employee engagement with a social networking firm, learned how important this is even in situations where the rewards are tangible. He was looking to boost the level of supportive communication he had with employees. In previous years, he presented the annual stock options to his direct supervisors and requested that they do the same with their direct reports. He decided to take a more personalized, different approach. Wanting to thank folks directly, he asked his direct supervisors if they'd mind him meeting with each of their employees who would receive stock options. They thought it was a terrific idea. Alan shared:

> I personally thanked them for the *specific* projects and their work. Employees were surprised that I would take the time out of my busy schedule to sit down with each of them separately, have a cup of coffee, and discuss their accomplishments. One of my supervisors later informed me that her employee appreciated *my time with her* more than she valued the stock options!

To encourage the heart well, you have to be personally involved, making the interaction personal with the individual or team being recognized, appreciated, and celebrated.

REFLECT ON
PERSONALIZING RECOGNITION

Ask Yourself:

1. Do I know enough about my key constituents (e.g., direct reports, peers I regularly interact with, key clients, and critical suppliers) to recognize them in a way they would appreciate?
2. Do I know enough about the various cultures in my workplace to express appreciation and provide recognition appropriately?
3. Have I been doing enough to personalize my recognition and appreciation of others? What more could I be doing?
4. How can I be more imaginative and creative in recognizing others?
5. How am I demonstrating that I care about the work, the product or service, and the people doing it?
6. Am I devoting enough time to ensuring that people don't think they and their work are being taken for granted?
7. What can I do to be better at catching people doing things right?

CHAPTER 8

The Fifth Essential

Tell the Story

In the new world of business, where it's every executive's job to make sense of a fast-changing environment, storytelling is the ultimate leadership tool.

—*ELIZABETH WEIL*
Simple Stories for Leadership Insight in the New Economy

TODAY, THE AUTHOR Stephen King is a household name. He's published more than sixty books and is one of the world's most successful writers, with many film adaptations of his novels and short stories. But he didn't start out as a success. If not for the encouragement and belief of his wife, Tabitha, he might have given up on writing altogether. "My wife made a crucial difference during those two years I spent teaching at Hampden," Stephen told the *Guardian*. "If she had suggested that the time I spent writing stories was wasted time, I think a lot of the heart would have gone out of me."

Stephen juggled working full-time and writing creatively when he had a lightning bolt of an idea for a book. This supernatural horror novel centered on adolescent cruelty and telekinesis:

I did three single-spaced pages of a first draft, then crumpled them up in disgust and threw them away.

The next night, when I came home from school, Tabby had the pages. She'd spied them while emptying my waste basket, had shaken the cigarette ashes off the crumpled balls of paper, smoothed them out, and sat down to read them. She wanted me to go on with it, she said. She wanted to know the rest of the story. I told her I didn't know [anything] about high school girls. She said she'd help me with that part. She was smiling in that severely cute way of hers. "You've got something here," she said. "I really think you do."[1]

He finished the manuscript. *Carrie* went on to become a bestseller, was adapted into a film starring Sissy Spacek, and launched Stephen King's writing career into the stratosphere. And it might never have happened without the encouragement of Tabitha King, who believed in her husband's ability and told him so. Nothing had changed in Stephen's ability to write between throwing away those three pages and going on to complete the novel—nothing except knowing that someone else believed in his talent.

Stephen's narrative beautifully exemplifies what we previously discussed about the second essential (expect the best): the profound and positive influence of our belief in another's capabilities. It's a testament to the power of optimism and hope in shaping the outcomes of our interactions. The ability to tell stories is an essential leadership skill and helps leaders effectively navigate today's turbulent and uncertain times.

Shannon Dixon-Kheir told us about an experience with one of the fundraising team's newest members (David) at her organization on his first out-of-state trip to visit donors. While David had a reputation for being somewhat goofy and entertaining within the office, few colleagues had had the opportunity to witness his thoughtfulness, creativity, and reliability when working with donors. Shannon recalled that when she was taken on her own first out-of-state fundraising trip by her supervisor, he bought her a mug with the name of the city they visited on it to memorialize that milestone in her career. "To this day, it is the only coffee mug I use in the office," she said.

After her first out-of-state donor visitation trip with David, Shannon told him how much this gesture meant to her and how it had inspired her career. Then she surprised David with the same gift—a mug from the city they had visited together—and he "was overwhelmed and grateful." Shannon explained that she "wanted David to feel the same support and joys I did when moving forward in the direction of growth, no matter how big or small the steps." Shannon's experience became a story she passed down to David, and no doubt he would add his own experience as the next chapter in that story.

These stories also highlight another critical element in encouraging the heart. They show the power of storytelling as a means of persuasion. The story makes the principle come to life; it makes it authentic.

The Story is the Reality

The world of business and organizations loves to talk in numbers. We're all inundated with financial statements, income statements, balance sheets, and stock tables. Numbers are so prevalent that they have come to be accepted. But numbers are abstractions from reality; the *story* is the reality.

Storytelling is how lessons are passed along from generation to generation, culture to culture. The past is a parable; the future is a fable. Storytelling is *the* most basic form of communication—more prevalent and powerful than facts and figures. People also believe stories more than they believe numbers.

"Oh, come on," you say. "You've got to be kidding! You mean to say that stories are more believable than hard statistical data?" Yes, that seems to be the case. First, we offer the data, which seems ironic given our last point, but let's take a look.

Organizational sociologists have studied the impact of stories on MBA students, an often numbers-driven, highly competitive, skeptical audience. In one study, the persuasiveness of four methods of convincing the students that a particular company truly practiced a policy of avoiding layoffs were compared.[2] In one scenario, only a story was used to persuade people. In a second, students were presented with statistical data that showed that the company had significantly less involuntary turnover than its competitors. Both the statistics and the story were used in the third scenario. At the same time, in the fourth, students were presented with a straightforward policy statement by an executive of the company.

Which method do you think was most believable: (1) story only, (2) statistics only, (3) statistics and story, or (4) policy statement? The answer is, as you've probably anticipated, the story only. The students in the groups that were given *only* the story believed the claim about the policy more than any other group. They also remembered it better several months later. You might also have suspected that an executive delivering the policy statement was the least convincing. Even the best-written company statement is a poor substitute for a well-told story.

The renowned trial attorney Gerry Spence, who has never lost a criminal trial before a jury, says that "the strongest structure for any argument is *story*." He goes on to illustrate his point:

> Storytelling has been the principal means by which we have taught one another from the beginning of time. The campfire. The tribal members gathered around, the little children peeping from behind the adults, their eyes as wide as dollars, listening, listening. The old man—can you hear his crackly voice, telling his stories of days gone by? Something is learned from the story—the way to surround and kill a saber-toothed tiger, the hunt for the king of the mastodons in a far-off valley, how the old man survived the storm. There are stories of love, of the discovery of special magic potions, of the evil of the warring neighboring tribes—all learning of man has been handed down for eons in the form of stories.[3]

Isn't Gerry's story about stories an excellent example of the point that he's making? It puts the message in a context and makes it come alive. "Yes," you say at the end. "Yes, that *is* how I learn." This lesson was not lost on Hannah Nelson, who took it upon herself in her leadership development journey to tell more stories about the good deeds of others. In doing so, Hannah recognized that storytelling doesn't just celebrate achievements but also fosters a strong sense of unity and purpose within the team, inspiring greater collaboration and mutual support. Learning to weave actions into a cohesive and compelling story gave her a deeper understanding of how storytelling can effectively inform, align, and inspire individuals toward achieving shared success.

While Hannah anticipated this would bring her closer to coworkers and further develop their self-esteem, the experience also impacted her general worldview:

> When I took the time to put my team's contributions into a story, it forced me to reflect more deeply on their impact and the efforts they made that led to a positive outcome. Crafting these narratives shifted my perspective because I was now always in the mode of putting the pieces together and looking for important stories to tell. I couldn't help but notice the good deeds of others more often, even those of complete strangers. I noticed more positivity around me, if for no other reason than it was on my mind to notice it. What a wonderful side effect!

Our research backs up these experiences. We find a strong relationship between the frequency to which leaders are reported to be telling stories of encouragement about the excellent work of others and the level of personal commitment their direct reports indicate to the organization's success, as shown in Figure 8.1. More than half of the respondents who experience their leaders telling encouraging stories *very frequently* and *almost always* strongly agree that they are personally committed. The other benefit of telling stories is how this behavior is strongly linked with

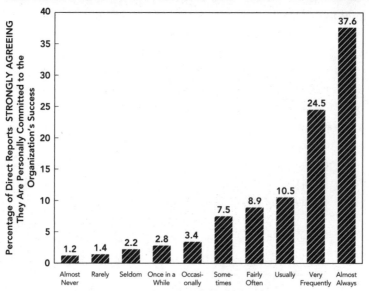

Figure 8.1 Personal commitment is built by leaders telling stories of encouragement.

the extent to which direct reports would recommend their leader to colleagues as a good leader. The results are depicted in this figure and closely mirror these findings.

Stories Teach, Mobilize, and Motivate

Storytelling has a remarkable ability to connect people and inspire them to do things they have never done before. When inundated with bits and bytes of information every nanosecond of every day, how can anyone possibly sort through it all and remember even a morsel? Research demonstrates that information is more quickly and accurately remembered when it is first presented as an example or story.[4] Researchers have found, for instance, that when American history textbooks were translated into the story-based style of *Time* and *Newsweek*, students could recall up to three times more information than they would after reading a more typical school text.[5] Similarly, scholars have contended that a good story is necessary to make sense of the often complex and contradictory decisions and events that go on daily in our organizations:

> The answer is something that preserves plausibility and coherence, something that is reasonable and memorable, something that embodies past experience and expectations, something that resonates with other people, something that can be constructed retrospectively but also can be used prospectively, something that captures both feeling and thought, something that allows for embellishment to fit current oddities, something that is fun to construct. In short, what is necessary in sense-making is a good story.[6]

The classic rational decision-making model in which people share opinions, generate alternatives, and make deliberate choices, is not how people make decisions in extreme emergencies (such as those faced by firefighters, critical care nurses, paramedics, pilots, nuclear plant operators, and battle planners). Instead, it has been shown in extreme emergencies how people use a nonlinear approach for decisions that involve intuition, mental simulation, metaphors, analogies, stories, and other less rational means—better known to most as "gut feelings." Indeed, one of the most potent methods for eliciting knowledge is to use stories.[7] Storytelling is an essential skill that leaders use to pass along the lessons that must be learned from highly complex, challenging situations.

Duane Nel, founder of a real estate firm with several hundred associates, explains that their industry is governed by clear rules. He never felt they needed to create a policy manual specific to the company. Instead, they passed along their values and standards by sharing stories: "We learned early on that people remembered, even cherished, the examples of what people did that really made a difference, whether it was going the extra mile to serve our customers or challenging the process in the pursuit of innovation and excellence. Not only did this improve camaraderie, but we found how in story form our values, standards, and examples of good behavior were easier to remember than if we had people memorize a set of policies."

You'll often hear leaders talk about needing a "new narrative" for their product, service, or organization that goes beyond simply stating, "This is what we do." Narratives are similar to storytelling, aiming to inspire employees and attract customers. Commitment and motivation are enhanced when we can see ourselves in the narrative. For example, Starbucks's origin story is that CEO Howard Schultz, while traveling through Europe, noted that in every country, there was a place between home and work where people gathered for conversation and community over a beverage.[8] Howard envisioned that Starbucks could be that "third place," and today, there are more than 38,000 locations worldwide.

Stories can motivate and mobilize better than bulleted points on an overhead. Well-told stories reach inside people and pull them along. They give an actual experience of being there and learning what is really important about the experience. Find ways that you can connect people with stories. Stories can also most effectively communicate higher meaning and "transcendent" purpose—for example, by describing how your colleague's actions solved the frustrating situations and problems of actual customers and, subsequently, how their quality of life was enhanced due to your product or service. When you can get people to empathize with the pain the customer experiences, they will also feel the pleasure of its resolution—all the more so if some heroics went into reducing suffering or producing joy.

Stories also play a pivotal role in changing and aligning an organization's culture with its strategy. Researchers examined how business leaders around the world approached this challenge. They discovered that successful leaders didn't begin with workshops, studies, or new HR policies:

> They began by creating stories highlighting actions that were deeply inconsistent with a firm's established culture but reinforced an alternative culture more aligned with its strategies. The most effective stories were authentic, featured the leaders themselves, offered a break with the past and a path to the future, appealed to hearts and minds, and were dramatic and memorable. Most critically, they empowered employees to begin crafting their own stories about cultural change so that everyone in the organization ended up co-creating a new culture together.
>
> Crafting new stories forces business leaders to commit to cultural change in a way that creating new HR policies or cultural charters doesn't. Once the stories have spread throughout an organization, they're difficult to disavow or dislodge. And as the new stories replace narratives that reinforce the old culture, employees begin coming up with their own stories and end up co-creating a new one consistent with a firm's strategies.[9]

Stories can alter broader attitudes outside of the workplace. Typically, messages that feel like commands are not received well; if you feel like you are being pushed into a corner, you're more likely to resist and feel like pushing back in return. But if someone tells you a story about a difficult situation or dilemma that they faced, the information will likely come across less like a lecture and more like a personal truth in the form of advice. Studies have shown that people receive more effective input when asking for advice rather than feedback.[10] Anecdotes can make health advice, for example, more personally salient and compelling. When people hear or read that someone with whom they identify has taken up meditation, for example, they are more prone to stick with it themselves.[11]

Research on how the brain works indicates that "stories are an effective way to transmit important information and values from one individual or community to the next. Personal and emotionally compelling stories engage more of the brain, and thus are better remembered."[12] Stories stimulate people's emotions, activating parts of the brain that are associated with empathy. Knowing someone's story—for example, where they come from, what they do, what they like, and things you might have in common—provides the groundwork for forming relationships.

Great Leaders are Great Storytellers

Because storytelling is so crucial to learning, sense-making, decision-making, motivating, and mobilizing, it's no wonder that we and other leadership researchers have stressed how compelling storytelling is as a leadership tool. In telling a story, you inevitably share a piece of yourself, if only by noting that you choose to tell this story rather than another. In doing so, scholars note that "you start to build trust and connect in new ways with your listeners. . .stories humanize you as a leader and allow you to *encourage the heart* of your team."[13]

After doing extensive research on the development of human intelligence, Harvard University professor of education Howard Gardner contended:

> The artful creation and articulation of stories constitutes a
> fundamental part of the leader's vocation. Stories speak to
> both parts of the human mind—its reason and emotion. And
> I suggest, further, that it is *stories of identity*— narratives that
> help individuals think about and feel who they are, where they
> come from, and where they are headed—that constitute the
> single most powerful weapon in the leader's literary arsenal.[14]

Building on Howard's work, other leadership scholars observe that the hallmark of exemplary leaders is their "ability to weave together all of what is happening in the organization into a vibrant story and, through the story (or narrative), lead their organizations into the future."[15] Research has shown that storytelling has a remarkable ability to connect people and inspire them to take action. "Our species thinks in metaphors and learns through stories," the anthropologist Mary Catherine Bateson wrote. Tim O'Brien, who has won acclaim for his books about the Vietnam War, put it this way: "Storytelling is the essential human activity. The harder the situation, the more essential it is."[16] When your organization needs to make a big change, stories will help you convey not only why it needs to transform but also what the future will look like in specific, vivid terms.

Stories are crucial to leading organizations into the future and equally important in encouraging people to continue the quest toward an elusive future, especially in times of great challenge and turmoil. The climb to the top is arduous and steep, and we all need encouragement to continue the ascent. Stories are essential means of conveying that progress is being made and that the actions people are taking are enabling them to get there.

Even giving someone the tools to reframe the story of challenges can positively impact performance in your organization. Ava DuVernay, the filmmaker of *Selma* and *A Wrinkle in Time* and the first Black female director to be nominated for a Golden Globe Award for Best Director, shared how her mentor, Oprah, helped her reframe the stories she tells herself about challenges:

> I was having a problem with something, and I said something like, "Why is this happening to me? Why me?" and she said, "This is not happening *to* you, this is happening *for* you."
>
> It really changed the way I think about every, every, every single thing. In traffic, white-knuckling it, trying to get to the meeting: *Why is there traffic on the way?* It's not happening to me, it's happening for me. [Now when that happens, I think] You need to slow down and you need to take a minute to prepare for where you're going to go. . . . Really thinking of it as your life is unfolding the way it's supposed to go, and it's all working for your good, even when it feels like a setback. It's a major shift.[17]

Stories, whether epics or vignettes, put a human face on life's lessons. They tell you that someone just like you can impact people and events. They create organizational role models that everyone can relate to. They put behavior in a real context. Stories touch and move people, making values and standards come alive.

Roxanne Armstrong has experienced firsthand the power of sharing stories, not just her own. As a division sales manager with a global software company, she has people share stories at their weekly meetings about what's working (especially) and even what seems problematic. "We celebrate," she says, "and we also learn and challenge each other as a team." Stories illustrate what everyone must do to live by the organization's standards. As Roxanne has learned, having people share their stories communicates the specific and proper actions needed to make a difference and resolve tough choices.

It's interesting to note that the word *story* is short for the word *history*. Both words have the same root and fundamentally mean the same thing. A story is a narrative of an event or series of events, just like history. Coincidentally, as we pointed out earlier, the word *recognition* means "knowing again." In a very real sense, recognition *is* a story. Telling stories can create a shared understanding of where people came from, who they are, and what they are capable of becoming. That's why telling the story is essential to recognizing someone for doing the right thing and doing things right.

How to Tell a Great Story

A good story is a blend of several ingredients:[18]

- ▶ Agents: the people who figure in the story
- ▶ Predicament: the problem the agents are trying to solve
- ▶ Intentions: what the agents plan to do

- ▶ Actions: what the agents do to achieve their intentions
- ▶ Objects: the tools the agents use
- ▶ Causality: the effects (both intended and unintended) of carrying out the actions
- ▶ Context: the many details surrounding the agents and actions
- ▶ Surprises: the unexpected things that happen in the story

Let's apply this framework to a recognition story and see how applicable it is. To do this, we go back to the story that began our discussion of the seven essentials of encouraging the heart, the one Tom Melohn told about Kelly. (To refresh your memory, you can reread it in its entirety in Chapter 2.)

- ▶ Is there an agent in Tom's story? Yes, Kelly is the agent.
- ▶ Predicament? Kelly is faced with the problem of figuring out what to do with two components that won't fit together. He's also faced with the prospect of rejecting a part in a "no-reject" culture. If he throws away the part, he is not meeting the standard. You can almost get inside Kelly's head from Tom's storytelling. You can imagine Kelly saying to himself, "If I throw these components out, then it will mean that they'll be scrapped. That violates our standard of 'no rejects.' What can I do so that I don't waste them?"
- ▶ Intentions? It's clear from the rest of the story that Kelly intended to get the rod and cylinder to fit together and ensure he lived up to the standard of no rejects. Kelly told Tom (and he told the gang) that he had imagined the inventive idea of putting the metal rod in the freezer to see if it would shrink.
- ▶ Actions? Kelly tried out his idea. He put the rod in the freezer.
- ▶ Objects? A freezer and two metal components: a rod, and a cylinder.

▶ Causality? "It worked." The effect of the action was that the rod and cylinder fit together, and the no-rejects standard was maintained.

▶ Context? The recognition occurred in the setting where the incident occurred: right there on the plant floor. Tom even brought the freezer into the story through his reenactment. Not only did Tom tell the story, but he also reenacted it. It was more than a story; it was almost a play.

▶ Surprises? Putting the metal rod in the freezer was out of the ordinary. Additionally, Tom's reenactment during the ceremony itself was full of surprises.

Try constructing a story like this the next time you are about to engage in an act of recognition. Here are some practical guidelines:

1. **Identify the actors.** Ensure that you have a person in mind you're trying to recognize. If there is more than one person involved—a team, for instance—name all the actors. Don't just say "the folks in accounting" or "the national account managers." Name names.

2. **State the predicament.** Present both the problem to be solved *and* the standard at stake. Don't pass up the chance to remind people of the values and principles involved in this situation. While praising people for solving a problem is one thing, praising them for living up to the organization's beliefs is more powerful.

3. **Clarify the actor's intentions.** In your recognition story, relate what went through the person's mind as they weighed their options. Of course, you'll have to talk to them about the incident to do this. This goes back to the essential of paying attention. You can't tell a good story if you don't pay attention.

4. **Describe the actions.** Relate what happened in as much detail as you can. What did the person do, specifically? If you can, reenact the process. Describing the behaviors is essential because the next time others face a similar predicament, they can recall "what Kelly did." They have a model of the kind of action they ought to take. The actions that they do take may not be precisely those that someone else did, but at least they have a framework for action.

5. **Include the props.** Like props in a play, objects are critical to a story. They give it detail and help people imagine themselves in the predicament. Objects may be inanimate or animate, and natural elements may be involved. This is your opportunity to add richness to the story, to make it come alive with detail.

6. **Tell how it ended.** Please don't leave the audience hanging; tell them the punch line. Tell the listeners what happened and why it made a difference.

7. **Paint—or reenact—the scene.** Be sure to place all of this in context. Relate where and when it happened. Talk about the surrounding circumstances. Set the stage; paint the scene. Again, it would be even more powerful, if possible, to take people to where it occurred.

8. **Include a surprise.** Every great story includes some element of surprise. Find a way to add an element of amazement. It adds interest, makes the story more memorable, and produces greater enjoyment. It might even get a laugh.

Recognition stories that include all these elements require time and preparation. Good storytelling is an art; like any art, it requires practice. But if you accept that storytelling is an effective leadership tool—as we've learned it is—then practice and preparation is well worth the investment.[19] Research has shown that employees who can tell many stories about their organization, especially positive ones, tend to be more committed and resilient from hardships than those with few stories to relate to.[20] This is true even for children, as storytelling boosts their self-esteem, improving their resiliency and interpersonal skills in dealing with hard times.[21]

What about Technology?

Storytelling is best experienced live and in person. It's the best way to sense the emotions of the storyteller and the audience truly. Body language, tone of voice, excitement, suspense, and surprise are felt more intensely. And yet performing live and in person is not always feasible. Distance, hybrid and virtual work, and a pandemic can make that impossible.

Fortunately, technological advancements now enable leaders to "be there" virtually. Just remember how quickly people pivoted to using Zoom during COVID-19. At the end of 2019, there were 10 million daily meetings on Zoom, and these days there are more than 300 million daily meetings on that platform.[22] Other online meeting platforms increase this number multifold. Technology, in other words, enhances our capacity to publicly recognize people and tell stories that acknowledge them for actions exemplifying the values and vision of the organization and bringing more meaning to people's lives.

Stories about your colleagues' triumphs at work can be communicated with the magic of technology. You can share several examples of what a departmental colleague did that was above and beyond the call of duty every week on your email system at work. The same can be done through voicemail or postings on social media platforms like Facebook or Slack; these technologies are available to everyone. Social media with video components—including Instagram and YouTube—are perfect opportunities to flex new storytelling modes and share positive contributions from your organization.

The beauty of social media is that stories can be told from so many perspectives: You can tell stories about your people's positive contributions, offer direct reports the opportunity to tell stories about what they've seen colleagues doing well, or even call for customers to share the stories from your organization that have positively impacted their lives. Low-tech or high-tech cultures of caring and support are built story by story, and fortunately, there are numerous media available for the telling.

REFLECT ON
TELLING THE STORY

Ask Yourself:

1. How long has it been since I told a story about someone who did something extraordinary in my organization?
2. How can I share more stories publicly than I am now doing? What's holding me back from doing this?
3. What must I do to make storytelling a tradition in my team and organization?
4. What stories are told most often in my organization? Are they communicating the right lessons and values?
5. How well do the often-told stories meet the criteria of a good story?
6. Are there values and lessons that should be more often communicated? What other stories should be told?
7. What can I do to improve my storytelling capability?

CHAPTER 9

The Sixth Essential

Celebrate Together

Celebration is an important opportunity to cement the lessons learned on the path to achievement, and to strengthen the relationships between people that make future achievement more plausible.

—WHITNEY JOHNSON
Smart Growth: How to Grow Your People to Grow Your Company

ALL OVER THE world, people celebrate. They take time off work to gather to mark an important occasion. They march in elaborate parades down the city's main street to shower a championship team with cheers of appreciation. They set off fireworks to commemorate great historic victories or the beginning of a new year. They convene impromptu ceremonies in the company conference room to toast the award of a new contract. They attend banquets to show respect for individuals and groups who've accomplished an extraordinary feat. They get all dressed up in tuxedos and gowns—and sometimes in very silly costumes—to rejoice at the passing of another season. They sit down at elaborate feasts to give thanks for the bountiful harvest. They get together with colleagues at the end of a grueling work session and give each other high-fives for a well-done job. And in tragic times, people come together in eulogy and song to honor those who showed courage, conviction, and sacrifice.

Why do people take time away from work to come together, tell stories, and raise their spirits? Celebrations are among the most significant ways people proclaim respect and gratitude, renew a sense of community, and remember shared values and traditions. They are also as important to an organization's long-term health as the daily performance of tasks.

Sometimes celebrations are elaborate affairs, but often they are individual recognitions that are turned into opportunities for group participation. One of our colleagues, Lori Heller, tells a story of a recognition-turned-celebration in her parents' small furniture factory. During the Christmas rush, her father always hired extra workers, and because they were temporary hires, motivation was often a problem. One day, her dad installed a "Bragging Board" at the entrance where employees hung up their coats. Whenever he wanted to acknowledge an employee for an achievement, he wrote them a quick thank you note and pinned it to the Bragging Board for all to see.

People appreciated the notes, of course, and, not surprisingly, they were left pinned to the board in public view rather than taken down and stored in a private place. Others started attaching their own notes to the board, announcing achievements and even family events outside of work that they wanted to brag about. Soon, notes such as "I'm a grandma! First one!" appeared on the board, usually with a photo of the new baby. One proud parent even pinned up a perfect report card that her son brought home from school. The Bragging Board, said Lori, "helped to create a sense of community and camaraderie. It said this factory was a place where your humanness mattered."

The Bragging Board also demonstrates that people love to *participate* in sharing and celebrating achievements and special milestones in their lives. Bragging boards have become so popular that you can find scores of options at online retailers like Etsy and Pinterest.

A Culture of Celebration

Scholarly research has shown that celebration influences performance. In one study, for example, the investigators found that what distinguished high-performing groups from those performing less well was the wide variety and frequency of celebratory events—events where recognition and appreciation were expressed.[1] In *Corporate Celebration: Play, Purpose, and Profit at Work,* the authors contend that celebration:

> is an integral element of culture [and] provides the symbolic adhesive that welds a community together. But there's more than that. Without transition, ritual, and ceremony, businesses cannot adjust to changing circumstances. In many different ways, celebration serves as an organization's heart. This is an alternative to the view that an organization's brain—information, analysis, and strategy—is the core.[2]

Organizations are now taking this message quite seriously. Celebrations and workplace fun have become part of many organizations' cultures. Hang around them long enough and you'll find many examples of how leaders celebrate together. We've witnessed a senior executive ride in on an elephant wearing a sultan's costume to celebrate a new product launch and another who invites high performers to his home, where he cooks dinner, plays his guitar, and sings. After completing a major acquisition, one senior leadership team created and widely shared a video where they performed a skit with singing, dancing, and a few jokes (mostly making fun of themselves). In another situation, key milestones and anniversaries were celebrated by whisking away employees (including spouses, partners, and guests) to an all-inclusive resort for a weekend. We were invited to accompany the engineering group to a local minor league baseball game, which began with a BBQ at the park and the chance to stand up and brag about the efforts and contributions of their colleagues in the group.

Are these too elaborate for you? How about taking a cue from organizations we've observed where they use stuffed giraffes as reminders that you often need to stick your neck out to ensure that you're doing the right things, not simply doing things right? At a company picnic, the executive team handles all the food service as just one way of thanking and honoring all those who nourished others day-to-day. In one office, whenever a win was achieved, they wheel out an ice cream cart, inviting people to enjoy a treat while sharing success stories. Other companies have committed to contributing to their communities by giving employees paid time off to work with social service organizations or participate in disaster relief activities. There are also awards banquets, appreciation lunches, and coffee breaks to give out spot awards.

Unsurprisingly, an organization with a reputation for being "a fun place to work" is becoming a factor in attracting, recruiting, and retaining employees.[3] Organizations that celebrate show they care for people, and that's the environment in which people want to work. With demographic shifts and changing expectations in the workforce, a "fun place to work" has become more than gimmicks and perks. According to one study, "Building meaningful work in a nurturing environment filled with growth opportunities underpinned by supportive management and trusted leadership is increasingly a must-have for organizations that want to thrive."[4]

To some, this culture of celebration might seem like a wasteful distraction. The Scrooges would say, "We haven't got time for fun and games. This is a fast-paced industry, and we can't stop production for things like that. After all, this is a business." Sure enough, however, promoting a culture of celebration fuels a sense of unity and purpose essential for retaining and motivating today's employees.

Yet it is so much more than that.

We Want to Involve Others in Our Lives

The need for affiliation is what motivates people to celebrate. People need people, and they want others to share in their lives and want to share in theirs. Otherwise, we'd all be hermits. Remember that celebration is an experience; in the workplace, it is most meaningful when shared with colleagues. Here's a little experiment you can try to find out how true this is.

Take a tour of your facility as soon as you can. We know you've done it before, but this time take a tour to notice what people have sitting on their desks, stuck to their bulletin boards, or hung on the walls. Who or what are in those picture frames? A loved one, a family pet, a special friend? What awards or diplomas are visible? What paintings and posters do you see? What trophies or tributes are sitting out? What do they celebrate? What do they signify? By the way, you can often do the same in a video conference; even the choice of a background screen reveals something about someone's interests and preferences. Take the time to engage folks in conversation about what you see.

Have you ever asked yourself why people put all these things on public display? Have you ever asked yourself why *you* put things on public display? Okay, sure, they do it for themselves. People like to remind themselves of accomplishments, the places they've been, and the people they love. People want to experience the emotions of joy, wonder, love, inspiration, importance, and success again. They want to *feel* something. Even—or especially—at work.

People display their mementos because they want to involve others in their lives. The photos, posters, and plaques invite people to join them in their experience. They say, "Here's something important to me. Here's something that gives me joy and meaning. Ask me about it." If people didn't want others to share these experiences, they would keep them hidden and secret. What is public is meant to be shared.

For example, prominently displayed on one of our colleague's consulting company's office walls is a poster of a multicolored striped zebra with a caption that reads, "To be good is not enough when you dream of being great." It's hung on the office wall not simply because it was eye-catching but to share an essential message about the company's culture and promise to its clients. In that organization, people love to talk about the zebra poster to anyone who asks—and to many who don't! As their managing partner told us, "We want to engage people in a conversation about what is meaningful and important to us, and the poster starts a conversation. If we kept it private, we'd miss an opportunity for dialogue, teaching, and fun."

What if, when you take the tour, you find no photos, mementos, or remembrances? What if the organization frowns on such personal displays? What if your company's culture discourages people from getting close to each other? If this is true, you should be very concerned, as a leader and human being, because what is at stake is not just work; it's your health and that of others.

Intimacy Heals; Loneliness Hurts

We said it at the beginning of this book, and we'll repeat it: the best leaders want to get closer to and be more personal with others than the poorer performers. Research also documents that these leaders are not only more likely to be successful but also more likely to be healthy. Strong social bonds lead to healthier, happier lives. Equally important, these leaders are more likely to promote the well-being of others.

Dean Ornish, MD, is a clinical professor of medicine and a world-renowned researcher in coronary heart disease. He wrote a groundbreaking work on the healing power of intimacy.[5] In his book *Love and Survival*, Dean reviewed many scientific studies that examined the impact of love and intimacy on a person's health and well-being. From his analysis, he concludes, "When you feel loved, nurtured, cared for, supported, and intimate, you are much more likely to be happier and healthier. You have a much lower risk of getting sick and, if you do, a much greater chance of surviving."[6] If you do not have anyone you feel close to, no one who'd take care of you, no one you could turn to in time of need, "you may have *three to five times* higher risk of premature death and disease from all causes"[7] (emphasis in original).

What Dean refers to as love, others refer to as social support. Studies on social isolation, social support, and intimacy have been conducted across the United States and worldwide. They've been done involving old, middle-aged, and young men and women.[8] If you're interested—or skeptical—review the evidence yourself. It'll make you smile, and it'll make you weep. It also makes you stop and think about the quality of your own relationships. All the evidence points in the same direction. Again, here's Dean:

> When I reviewed the scientific literature, I was amazed to find what a powerful difference love and relationships make on the incidence of disease and premature death from virtually *all* causes. It may be hard to believe that something as simple as talking with friends, feeling close to your parents, sharing feelings openly, or making yourself vulnerable to others in order to enhance intimacy can make such a powerful difference in your health and well-being, but study after study indicates that they often do.[9]

It turns out that the quality of relationships has a protective effect. The more cohesive, supportive, and loving relationships are, the healthier the immune system is and the more resistant one is to disease. Although it does help to have several close social relationships, even one is significantly better than none. You can have the best job in the world and make more money than anyone, but if you lack close social ties, you may not live to enjoy it. Various studies have shown that increased social contact can boost morale and productivity. In one study, call center employees were divided into two groups: one taking staggered fifteen-minute breaks solo and the other taking breaks with their coworkers.

Those who had an opportunity to chat and socialize showed a 20 percent performance increase.[10]

High-performing teams have been found to invest considerable time in bonding over nonwork topics (e.g., books, sports, streaming shows and films, and family) due to meeting and spending time with their colleagues informally (e.g., sharing a break). People identify shared interests in these interpersonal conversations, fostering more profound and authentic relationships. Consequently, members of high-performing teams express more positive emotions with their colleagues, giving and receiving appreciation more frequently and feeling psychologically safe to share disagreements and alternative perspectives.[11]

All this evidence, and more, is supported by findings from the longest longitudinal study of human thriving, the Harvard Study of Adult Development. It's been going on for more than eighty-five years and has been the subject of hundreds of papers and related research studies. The authors of the most recent book on the study report that if they had to boil down the years of research into one principle for living, it would be: "Good relationships keep us healthier and happier. Period."[12] They assert, "Positive relationships are essential to human well-being."[13]

A healthier life is the precious gift that leaders give when they bring people together, build positive relationships, and provide social support. Based on the empirical evidence and now with the increase in remote and hybrid work, it is not going too far to say that leaders who effectively use social support activities promote higher performance levels and reduce death and disease. Now, think about what that means to the organization's bottom line: celebrations are quite literally life-giving forces.

Joseph Leamon, vice president of sales and marketing for one of Napa Valley's premier wineries, has seamlessly built a community spirit by hosting celebrations and encouraging friendships such that all his employees are eager to help one another out under any circumstances. He hosted team dinners after hours, personally wrote notes of appreciation, and made a point to recognize employee contributions frequently and creatively. At dinners, for example, Joseph had everyone share their favorite hospitality story from the winery, and then they would vote for their favorite. The winner typically left with a special bottle of wine. His staff said these team dinners and celebrations "encouraged us to build relationships and make friends." Another team member told us that Joseph never failed to take an opportunity to tell his team they were amazing and could do great things:

> He drew us in with his kind heart and showed that he genu-inely loved and cared for every one of us. When I was frus-trated with a project that I had been putting a lot of extra hours into, he told me, 'I know you can do this. It's why I hired you. But one thing to remember is that no one will die if the project isn't perfect. This is supposed to be fun.' I was driven to do a good job. I wanted to make him proud of my work because he believed in me. We were all motivated to perform and dedi-cated to our jobs because we felt like a family, always willing to chip in and help someone out when they needed support. No one wanted to let Joseph down.

Letting people know, as Joseph did, that you appreciate them and are grateful for what and how they do their work also directly impacts their willingness to reach out and help others. Consider the findings from this study where participants who had edited a student's cover letter received either a neutral message from the student acknowledging they'd received their feedback or a grateful note expressing thanks and appreciation. When these participants were asked for additional assistance, those who were thanked were twice as likely to say yes than those who hadn't been thanked.[14] Alternatively, you will unlikely continue offering help when you are not thanked or appreciated.

Don't forget the importance of creating community among remote employees, making sure they don't feel isolated and invisible because not feeling a sense of belonging is among the strongest predictors of low morale and turnover. Watch for the "out of sight, out of mind" trap when recognizing those working remotely. While you may be unable to interact with them informally and offer a spot gesture of appreciation, consider communicating nondigitally; for example, sending them a postcard or even a physical package, reminding them that their work is not taken for granted.[15] Create time and space (virtual or physical) for people to express their gratitude and recognize one another's efforts and achievements. Provide time at the beginning of virtual team meetings for people to express their appreciation and gratitude.

Celebrations Build Community

Celebrations—recognizing one person's accomplishment or cheering the achievements of many—are opportunities to promote individual well-being and for leaders to build healthier groups. Providing highly visible public recognition builds the recipients' self-esteem and a sense of community and belonging, of working together to achieve shared goals and victories. One analysis finds:

> Celebrations infuse life with passion and purpose. . . . They bond people together and connect us to shared values and myths. Ceremonies and rituals create community, fusing individual souls with the corporate spirit. When everything is going well, ritual occasions allow us to revel in our glory. When times are tough, ceremonies draw us together, kindling hope and faith that better times lie ahead.[16]

As members of your organization interact on more than just a professional level, they're likely to come to know and care about one another. When you have a high level of participation not just in the work itself but in celebrating achievements, you reinforce people's common stake in reaching their goals. Making people feel included is a central function of any celebration, and the more people you can encourage through well-designed and participatory celebrations, the more your organization's people grow close. Everyone wants to feel part of the team, but it's even more important to feel part of something larger than yourself.

Public recognition—such as awarding certificates during a team meeting—can motivate the entire team. Public recognition can not only feel more impactful to the recipient, but it can also boost motivation among all employees, including those who aren't recognized themselves.[17] When thank-you cards were publicly awarded to the three top performers in small work groups, researchers found that performance increased not just for the top performers who received the recognition but also for all group members.[18] Witnessing a colleague receive accolades can motivate others to measure up and improve their performance.

Participating in celebrations increases the sense of belonging and esprit de corps. In particular, participatory celebrations bring people together so that information can be exchanged, relationships can be nourished, and a sense of shared destiny can be sustained. By making achievements public, you encourage the person being recognized and the hearts of those who witness the award. You build a culture where people feel they are appreciated and applauded. People who count themselves as members of this "community" can find meaning and purpose here.

Besides, knowing that you could probably be doing something else or be somewhere else, would you *want* to work for a place with no ritual or ceremony—a boring place celebrating nothing? Our colleague the late David Campbell, with the Center for Creative Leadership (who, by the way, assembled the world's most extensive private postcard collection!), so eloquently noted:

> A leader who ignores or impedes organizational ceremonies and considers them as frivolous or "not cost-effective" is ignoring the rhythms of history and our collective conditioning. [Ceremonies] are the punctuation marks that make sense of the passage of time; without them, there are no beginnings and endings. Life becomes an endless series of Wednesdays.[19]

So if you're tired of an endless series of Wednesdays, take time out to celebrate something. Listed below are some examples from organization development consultant Cathy DeForest of why you might celebrate:[20]

▶ *Organizational change and transition:* expansions, reorganizations, closings, mergers, the end of an old technology and the introduction of a new one, moves to new locations

▶ *Success:* financial success, promotions, awards, expansions to new markets

▶ *Loss:* of old procedures, financial opportunities, contracts, a job, status, a colleague who has just died, an experiment that ended in failure

▶ *People:* team successes, founders, winners of sales contests, employee awards, individual birthdays, marriages, reunions, doing good deeds for others

▶ *Events:* a company's anniversary, opening day, holidays, articulation of an organization's vision

▶ *The unknown:* paradox, ambiguity in the marketplace

Whatever you decide to celebrate and for whatever reason, do so knowing that as a leader, you are bringing more joy into people's lives and fulfilling one of the most essential functions of a leader. You are strengthening a sense of community and a team spirit that will infuse your organization with tremendous positive energy to face today's and tomorrow's challenges.

Celebrations Reinforce Values

Celebrations serve another critical function. They offer opportunities to reinforce organizational values. Whether in honor of individual, group, or organizational achievement, celebrations communicate what's important around your workplace. They broadcast for all to see and hear the principles that are important enough that time and money should be spent to recognize them.

Celebrations—public statements by their very nature—express and reinforce commitment to central values. They visibly demonstrate that the organization is serious about adhering to its principles. You must be clear about the statements you're making in any celebration. What are you reinforcing? What are you saying is significant about this moment? Parties are fine, but celebrations are more than parties. They're ceremonies and rituals that create meaning. When planning a celebration, every leader should ask, "What meaning am I trying to create?"

Public ceremonies crystallize personal commitments, binding people together and letting them know they're not alone. For example, when direct reports perceive that their leaders frequently and "publicly recognize people who exemplify a commitment to shared values," they report the most substantial feelings of team spirit, as shown in Figure 9.1. These results are very similar to those found when we asked about the extent to which people feel valued by their organization.

Success is reinforced when individuals or teams are singled out for recognition in a public event and held up as role models. Research shows that peers make better role models than those who are socially distant (e.g., several hierarchical levels above). People need to see the behavior of others to whom they can relate.

Public recognition allows leaders to convey, "Here's someone just like you. You can do this!" By publicly recognizing an individual whose actions represent the group's values, you give them much-appreciated thanks and provide their colleagues with an example they can emulate. They also see that one of their own is recognized for doing the right things and doing things right. They see that efforts to go the extra mile are appreciated.

Lisa Sones works with many scientists as a global biotech company's new product launch manager. She was quick and candid in telling us that public recognition and the idea of making it an intentionally structured practice did not feel natural for her. Still, she decided to give it a go and, like a scientist, set up an experiment to see what the

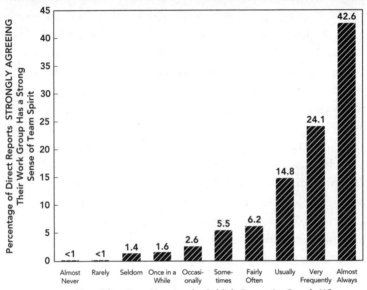

Figure 9.1 Team spirit increases as leaders publicly recognize people for their commitment to shared values.

difference between public versus private recognition and adding more intentional regularity to such recognition would yield for her team and herself.

She started a new habit of taking some time at the end of each week to think about the great work done by her team and used the reflections as a leadup to their Monday morning team meeting. Here is one of the first things she realized:

> This turned out to be a nice way for me to transition from the often-grinding work week into the weekend. More sig-nificantly, however, to my surprise, my sharing recognition with the broader group at team meetings was positively received and aligned with our values. In fact, it created a new

community practice for us. Now we always start our meetings with recognition. It sets a solid and positive tone and quickly pulls everyone into a safe, collaborative space, regardless of what they were dealing with before our time together.

You may be reluctant to recognize people in public and celebrate with others, fearing that doing so might cause resentment or jealousy. However, private recognition and rewards do little to set an example. Often the recipient, not wanting to brag or appear conceited, has no opportunity to share the story with others. Tell your constituents and colleagues that they've done well as soon as you find out about it, and let other people know about the accomplishment, too.

Public recognition also strengthens recipients by increasing their visibility and building a connection between people. Military organizations, for example, make tremendous use of medals and insignias, which are almost always handed out in ceremonies. Public recognition also builds commitment because it makes people's actions visible to their peers, and therefore difficult to deny or revoke.

What do you do about people who do not get recognized, such as someone whose performance is not especially recognized in a meeting or who did not receive an award for top performance? Will these people feel left out because they believe they deserve recognition? Will they feel hurt, offended, or slighted by this oversight? The fact of the matter is that if you are doing recognition well, you are including everyone who is deserving, so the concern is more along the lines of "What do I do about the people who are not deserving of recognition, public or otherwise?" The answer to this question is relatively simple: don't recognize them. Don't thank them for showing up to work when others have been working hard to get the results needed. Don't make them super-person-of-the-month just because they've been around longer than anyone who has received this award. Doing so will undermine your credibility and the role of recognition in your organization.

What do you do if someone comes and asks or complains about why they did not receive recognition for an achievement for which you praised someone else? The advice of a recognition guru, Bob Nelson, is to acknowledge that you may have made a mistake and correct it. After all, it is impossible to know everything that goes on.[21] For example, "Matt, tell me what you did, and if I overlooked that achievement, I apologize, and I will reference you in the next staff meeting." However, if recognition is not warranted, this will give you a chance to initiate a conversation with that individual about the situation. Such a discussion might create a greater understanding of priorities and a chance to start over with new performance goals and plans to attain them. For example, "Michelle, thanks for coming to talk with me about this. I want to be able to recognize your performance, but I haven't seen yet how it is merited. Would you be open to discussing what needs to be different for that to happen—and what I can do to help?"

Public recognition and celebrations provide opportunities to reinforce shared values and highlight those whose behaviors and actions align with them. In that process, leaders build community and hold up a mirror for everyone to see what they pay attention to and what it means to be exemplary individually and as a team.

Take Care of Yourself: Nurture Your Network

Earlier, we commented on the healing power of social support. This applies as much to you, the leader, as it does to your constituents. With times as challenging as they are, having a solid support network is absolutely essential. You may be the bastion of courage and hope for others during difficult times, but you don't work in a vacuum. You need support as much as the people you work with do.

Trying to get support from the group you support can sometimes be like pulling yourself up by the bootstraps. Particularly during stressful times, you must be able to turn to your friends outside work and peers within the world of work. You need people to support you regarding specific issues. If the world is closing in around you, and you don't have good support, there's no way you'll survive the pressure or distress you feel from the people around you. You can safely bet that this pressure and distress will be mirrored back to you in one form or another.

When the pressure is on, your personal support system can provide you with a place to let off steam and a forum for brainstorming solutions. Don't neglect or take the supportive relationships in your life for granted. If you do, the support those people can offer at a critical time may not be available. Pay particular attention to personal relationships in times of change or crisis. Whenever you feel the demands of striving for extraordinary accomplishment, you especially need these relationships to assist you. Whether coping with excessive stress or reaching deeper into your inner resources, friends and supporters are the medicine you need. Determine which relationships need to be strengthened or renewed and reach out and connect with those people.

If you're building an organization that encourages the heart in the ways we've discussed, the support you give others comes back to you. One sure sign that what you're doing is working is when you see that encouraging the heart is becoming everyone's responsibility. In many ways, what goes around comes around; leaders get back what they give. That's why setting an example is so important. We turn to this issue in the next chapter.

REFLECT ON
CELEBRATING TOGETHER

Ask Yourself:

1. How frequently do I celebrate accomplishments? Is that often enough?
2. Are there sufficient opportunities for people to socialize and get to know one another?
3. What can I do to make connections between people and facilitate networking?
4. When celebrating, are we intentionally linking to important values and standards?
5. How am I using public recognition and celebration to create role models for others in the organization?
6. How am I making our celebrations fun? Are they too routine, with inadequate surprises and prizes?
7. How supported do I feel in this organization? What can I do to nurture my network of colleagues and friends who can be there for me in my times of need?

CHAPTER 10

The Seventh Essential

Set the Example

Today is only one day in all the days that will ever be. But what will happen in all the other days that ever come can depend on what you do today.

—ERNEST HEMINGWAY
For Whom the Bell Tolls

WE BEGAN OUR discussion of the essentials of encouraging the heart by sharing stories and evidence about the importance of setting standards aligned with purpose. We return to that conversation because when striving to attain standards of excellence and distinction, you must recognize, reinforce, and celebrate exceptional efforts and successes that serve shared values and vision. The celebrations and recognitions should be authentic expressions of appreciation for the hard work and dedication of the people who live those values. You must get *personally* involved; if you want people to have the courage to continue the quest for excellence in the face of great adversity, you must set the example and encourage them yourself.

It's not one big celebration that makes the difference. It's small, thoughtful daily actions that show people you care. That is precisely what Beth Taute told us about Jo, the manager she worked with at a global financial institution. Jo led a small team of analysts responsible for upgrading the human resources system, involving more than 150,000 employees across more than fifty-two countries. From the beginning, Jo let people know in many different ways that she was there for them. Beth told us:

> Jo had taken on the task because she felt the team could do it. She shared her belief in the team's ability in their weekly meeting. She sat with each of them individually in one-to-one meetings to allow them to express their fears or reservations. She wanted each person in her team to feel that their opinions were important enough to be considered individually.

Jo got the ball rolling, and within a few days, the team was up to their necks in various systems and issues. They were rarely done with their work before midnight due to the tight time constraints placed on them, and Jo was always right alongside them. She even moved out of her office onto the floor to be closer to them, and they converted her office to a meeting room for the various conference calls they were making. She often had to leave the office early to pick her daughter up and take her home, but she'd always return with pizza, late-night snacks, or coffee for the team.

Jo would do other small things, like take the team offsite for a surprise lunch. She let team members leave early if she knew they had something special happening in the evening. She let team members with children come in late or leave early on special occasions like birthdays so that they could spend the morning or afternoon with them. Jo let her team know their hard work was appreciated with small, silly gifts with hidden jokes or meanings scattered on everyone's desks.

Jo knew the project was an enormous undertaking, and so did her team. Because of her hands-on personal involvement, her team wanted to show her that her confidence and trust in them were correctly placed by meeting and trying to exceed her expectations. She was their chief cheerleader and supporter. She was also their first line of help when they needed it and the biggest believer in their ability to succeed. Her enthusiasm for the project and their ability to complete it spilled over to the team. Beth summed up her experience with Jo this way:

> Jo made coming to work and being there late seem fun and not like a hard slog. I learned that leaders have to be involved and connected with what's going on and that the best recognition is ongoing, without being expected or predictable.

It's this kind of personal dedication and involvement that enables leaders to earn trust and respect and to teach the kinds of lessons that Beth learned about involvement, connection, and recognition. It's the same story over and over again. Wherever you find a strong culture built around shared values—whether about superior quality, innovation, customer service, distinctiveness in design, respect for others, hard work, or just plain fun—you also find endless examples of leaders who personally live the values.

It's certainly helpful if this starts at the top of the organization. We consistently hear the refrain from employees that "encouraging the heart emanates from the top." It can start with something as simple as a thank-you note. One consumer products executive we know about sent more than thirty thousand thank-you notes to his employees during his tenure.[1] Another CEO, wanting to demonstrate the power of gratitude, regularly sent more than four hundred thank-you notes each year to the parents of her senior team members, expressing appreciation for sharing their children with the firm. Many of her colleagues told reporters this was the nicest thing that had ever happened to them.[2] Senior leaders in an organization set the tone. Cultures of encouragement thrive when organizational leaders set an example that communicates the message "around here, we say thanks, show appreciation, and have fun."[3]

That said, a *culture* of encouragement can only be sustained over time when *everyone becomes a leader* and when everyone sets the example.

Steve Mugavin, customer success service manager with a global computer software company, was one leader who took this message to heart. He sought new ways to conscientiously express gratitude and acknowledgment through informal channels and recognize his team more frequently. He didn't realize the reciprocal nature in which doing so brought the team together:

> Once I started using open channels, such as Slack, to acknowledge individuals, it quickly spread like wildfire. Team members followed suit and began vocalizing their recognition of their colleagues. These simple acknowledgments quickly morphed from statements of praise into requests for cross-training and support. Team members began to lean on each other to help enable their performance improvement instead of coming to me. At the same time, this helped to fuel team members' education on new ideas and approaches to similar problems.

Steve's story illustrates another positive outcome of leaders setting the example of encouraging the heart. It's contagious. Expressing gratitude tends to catch fire and spread from one person to another. It can become a way of life in an organization where leaders and their team members model the importance and the process of showing their appreciation for positive contributions to individuals, groups, and organizations.[4]

Credibility is the Foundation

We keep relearning the lesson that it all starts with credibility. In our continuing research on the qualities that people look for and admire in their leaders, time and time again we find that, more than anything, people want credible leaders.[5] Credibility is the foundation of leadership. Period.

Above all, people want to believe in their leaders. They want to believe that the leader's word can be trusted and that they do what they say. Our findings are so consistent over such a long period that we've come to refer to this as the first law of leadership: if you don't believe in the messenger, you won't believe the message.[6]

Leadership credibility dramatically affects performance and commitment to an organization. We examined the attitudes and performance of people led by individuals who scored high on personal credibility and those led by individuals who scored low. Here's what we found.[7] When people perceive their immediate managers or the senior managers in their organization to have high credibility, they were significantly more likely to:

▶ Be proud to tell others they're part of the organization

▶ Feel a strong sense of team spirit

▶ See their values as consistent with those of the organization

▶ Feel attached and committed to the organization

▶ Have a sense of ownership of the organization

However, when people perceive their immediate managers to have low credibility, they're significantly more likely to:

▶ Produce only if they're watched carefully

▶ Be motivated primarily by money

▶ Say good things about the organization publicly but criticize it privately

▶ Consider looking for another job if the organization experiences problems

▶ Feel unsupported and unappreciated

Credibility makes a difference. Loyalty, commitment, energy, and productivity depend upon it.

So what exactly is credibility? What is it *behaviorally*? How do you know it when you see it in action? We asked these questions, and here are some of the things people told us in response:

- ▶ "Credible leaders practice what they preach."
- ▶ "They walk the talk."
- ▶ "Their actions are consistent with their words."
- ▶ "They put their money where their mouth is."
- ▶ "They keep their promises."
- ▶ The most frequent response: "They do what they say they will do."

When deciding whether a leader is believable, people first listen to the words and then watch the actions. They listen to the talk and watch the walk; then, they measure the congruence. If the two are consonant, a judgment of "credible" is handed down. If people don't see consistency, they conclude that the leader is, at best, not serious about what they say and, at worst, an outright hypocrite.

Deeds move constituents, and actions are the evidence of a leader's credibility. This observation leads to a straightforward prescription for leader modeling: DWYSYWD—do what you say you will do. Figure 10.1 shows that few direct reports would strongly agree that their leader is effective unless they are *very frequently* following through on the promises and commitments they make.

DWYSYWD has two essential elements: the first is *say,* and the second is *do*. To set an example, leaders must be clear about their values and what they stand for. That's the *say* part. Remember that our first essential to encouraging the heart is to set clear standards. We start there because we know that's where credibility begins. But words are not enough. Leaders must put what they say into practice, act on their beliefs, and *do*.

In the domain of leadership, however, DWYSYWD is necessary but insufficient. Doing what you say you will do may make you credible personally, but it may not make you a credible *leader*. Leaders represent

Figure 10.1 Effectiveness rating of leaders increase the more often they are observed *doing what they say they will do.*

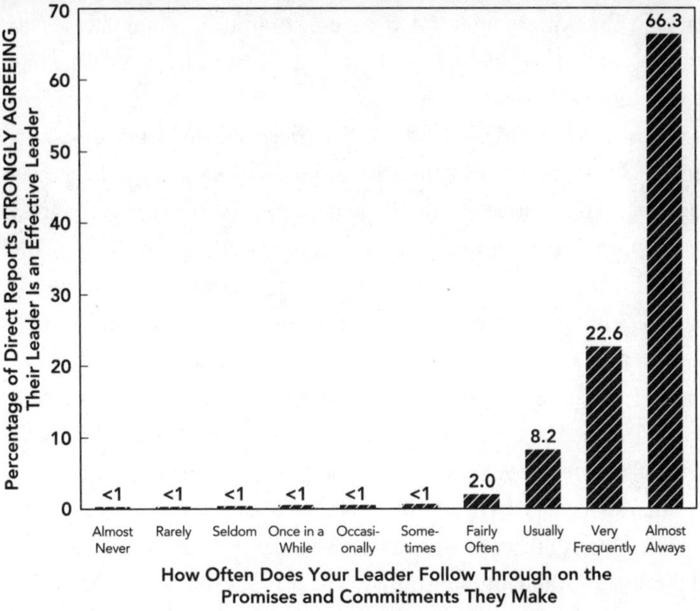

How Often Does Your Leader Follow Through on the
Promises and Commitments They Make

groups of people, and those constituents have needs and interests, values and visions. To set an example—and to earn and strengthen leadership credibility—if you want to be a leader you must base your actions on a *collective* set of aims and aspirations. That is: DWWSWWD. Do what *we* say *we* will do.

DWWSWWD reveals the essentials leaders must master to set an example and sustain leader credibility. We call it the "say-we-do" process, and it means that leaders must be able to:

▶ Clarify their own and others' values and beliefs.

▶ Unify constituents around shared values.

▶ Intensify their commitment to shared values by living them daily and reinforcing others' behavioral commitment.

If you want to create and sustain a culture of celebration and recognition, you've got to set the example. Your actions signal who you are and what you expect of others. Suppose your constituents can see and hear you thanking people for their contributions, telling stories about their accomplishments, and celebrating successes. In that case, chances are that they will do the same.

At one company we studied, the organization development team wanted to ensure that organizational leaders recognized the power of modeling. They founded the "Signal Corps," whose singular mission was to promote the importance of *examples* and *signals*. Their Signal Corps Creed pointed out how vital each encounter with employees was in impressing upon them the appropriate behaviors. Each encounter was seen as a moment of truth during which leaders could leave either a good or a bad impression. Signal Corps members pledged to be constantly mindful of creating a good impression consistent with organizational values. Their behavior, they knew, spoke louder than their words.

All leaders need to heed this creed. Nothing communicates a message more clearly than what the leaders do when spreading a message throughout the organization. Jumping out of an airplane or dressing in fancy clothes may not be your thing. That's not the point. The point is that directly and visibly showing others you're there to cheer them along sends a positive signal. You're more likely to see others do it if you do it. It's that simple.

You also have more credibility when you encourage others to encourage the heart. They're more likely to believe you are serious when it's not just about you but about how everyone should set an example. To excel as a leader, you must acknowledge that people believe what you do, not what you say.

It's All about Relationships

Denise Roundtree, a marketing and events manager whose company distributes anime, films, and television series, realized that "as much as each emerging leader wants to be a superhero in their organization, it is important to recognize that it takes a village to accomplish great things. There is only so much one person can humanly achieve no matter how much we try, and that's why it's important to trust others and be able to work with others." Denise told us about some incredible performances when teams had a strong sense of trust, and people felt connected, knowing they couldn't achieve greatness alone.

While you can find more than two hundred definitions of leadership in the academic literature, they can generally be reduced to simply asking, in behavioral terms, is anyone willing to follow you? While there are numerous reasons why people want to follow someone, the fundamental reason is that they believe that person cares about them and has their best interests at heart. They want to be in relationships where they are better off being in them than they would be otherwise (even though we can acknowledge that circumstances sometimes bind or shackle people in unhealthy ones). Leadership is a relationship involving those who would lead, connecting with those who would follow, and the foundation for building a relationship is predicated on trust.

In any relationship, personal or professional, it takes time to build trust. It often requires incremental steps of opening ourselves to another person, not knowing whether what we share will be understood, valued, and respected. A regional hospital administrator, Ron Perry, admitted that he did not know much about his colleagues—that his knowledge was "mostly limited to professional aspects." However, as he gradually opened up, sharing information about himself here and there, he noticed a shift occurring as his work colleagues embraced his openness. It wasn't a one-way street, either. Ron discovered that while he tended to be talkative, "I prioritized listening for a change, getting to know the other person, and learning about them. For instance, I discovered a shared interest in hiking with one of my work colleagues. Pleasantly, it lifted our team dynamic and spirit regarding work."

Connecting with others on a more personal level also sets an example for others to do the same, cultivating relationships among your team members. For instance, at every Friday's stand-up meeting, Ron set aside a time for team recognition, where team members talked about one person who helped them do their job better in the past week. Whether it was a short phone call for some help or hours of complex customer escalation debugging, it was, Ron said, "heartening to see team members being generous in their comments for others. Every story they shared boosted the team's trust level and strengthened our relationships."

You might call Ron's actions "team building," and you wouldn't be wrong—as long as you appreciate how such interactions foster relationships by encouraging the heart. There were times in his experience when the team failed to deliver on a project successfully. Even in those instances, Ron explained, "We celebrated the efforts put in by people, with lessons for everyone to know and acknowledge. We gave failure as much importance as our successes because we learned from them, and we'll start again with the resolve to do better." Even while interacting virtually, Ron had the team celebrate as if they were face-to-face. For example, they had lunch meetings wherein everyone got food ordered at the office expense and ate together over a video call. They played virtual video games, card games, and chess tournaments. These were just some of the ways, he told us, that relationships were nurtured and sustained.

Sarah Dunn thought she had mastered encouraging the heart as a leadership practice by "knowing my team and keeping a pulse on what works best for them." When she moved to a much larger school district as superintendent, she appreciated that she needed to "pay attention to what people here needed from me." While she relied on certain past behaviors, Sarah soon learned a valuable lesson:

> Certain members of my new team weren't looking for gift cards. They wanted more one-on-one time with me to continue building their relationship, create security in this new relationship, and get more coaching and feedback from me. Having learned from this experience, I strongly recommend diving deeper into getting to know the people you work with. Then you can be more thoughtful about recognizing them and their work.

Earlier in this chapter, we told you about Steve Mugavin's efforts to recognize team members more frequently. Another outcome of his efforts was that they fostered stronger relationships between himself and his team. Steve didn't realize "how encouragement and increased collaboration, at first, were correlated." At one of his employee feedback sessions, he learned about one of his direct reports' willingness to reach out to other team members, whom she had previously found intimidating. She attributed this change directly to the praise and respect for her performance at a recent engagement with another colleague. Steve shared:

> This confirmed that the simple practice of encouraging peers impacted the larger team's performance. It reinforced everything I was hoping this practice could be. It served as motivation to find more ways to reach out and connect with individuals. Still, more importantly, it reinforced that small gestures can significantly improve and strengthen relationships for everyone, whether directly or indirectly involved.

The foundation of any community is predicated on relationships. Developing strong social connections leads to more trust, reciprocity, information flow, collaborative action, productivity, and even happiness.

Start the Day With Encouragement

We can't think of a better way to start the day than to offer someone encouragement. Why not set a positive tone bright and early by expressing how much you appreciate the contributions of others?

Connie Lynch makes this part of her daily routine. As a product development manager, she created a daily appreciation reminder and screen saver on her computer screen, which pops up every morning and refreshes hourly. The reminder offers ways she might say thank you and show her appreciation to the people she works with. Connie occasionally adds to the list as she imagines and discovers new ways to encourage the heart. On it, she's listed possible rewards for individuals (from gift certificates to weekend getaways), ways to acknowledge group milestones (from an informal afternoon at the beach to an office party with award presentations), and even ideas for theme days to encourage camaraderie (e.g., Hawaiian or favorite sports team shirt days). She also keeps on hand several token and symbolic items for "spot recognitions," such as coffee mugs, gym bags, pen/pencil sets, giant candy bars, and stuffed animals. The screen saver reminds her (quite frequently) what she can do to recognize individual contributions and celebrate team accomplishments.

We love Connie's computer reminder. It illustrates the most fundamental principle of how people change their behavior: change happens only when you take a first step and then progress one step at a time. Connie decided to do more to recognize individual contributions and celebrate team accomplishments. She made herself a list so that every day there'd be something on it she could do. Another colleague of ours, Rob Finch, starts each day with three coins in his right-hand pants pocket, and each time he catches someone doing something right and lets them know about it, he moves a coin to his left pocket. This small step reminds him to encourage the heart and cheer on others in the organization.

You can find the word "cheerleader" in the dictionary, but the word you won't find is "cheer manager." It doesn't exist, and that's because you can't manage cheerleading. This point was sardonically illustrated in an editorial cartoon showing a manager talking to his subordinate, saying, "Pat, according to our management policy, you are just about due for a compliment." There's much more to cheerleading than standard shout-outs, acrobatics, and flashy routines. Foremost is being clear on the shared values and linking them to the recognition and celebration.

Amanda McKnight, like Connie, was all-in when it came to recognizing people on her team, but she wanted to extend encouragement to individuals outside of her immediate purview. "To say this was simple," Amanda told us, "was an understatement." She reviewed the company's internal newsletter and blog postings, and when she read about someone from her program, she forwarded them a personal message congratulating them on their accolades. Typically, this resulted in some back-and-forth of appreciation, which made the recipient of her message feel valued and helped Amanda foster closer ties with her colleagues. But what surprised her one day was a message from her director. He had connected with the individuals Amanda had reached out and told her:

> I really appreciate the very conscious effort you are making to recognize team achievements. I really like that you are expanding it beyond your own team. It can be very hard to keep up with all the kudos people deserve, but it's important, so it's much appreciated that you are visibly stepping up here. You've always done a good job highlighting others when you've been involved or in the peripheral, but I think it's great you are personally reaching out to celebrate beyond engagements you have immediate insight on.

Amanda told us that she "felt immense gratitude that my director had recognized my actions' intent and saw the merit in my behavior. I didn't expect how quickly it would motivate me to want to do more for the program." The empirical data bears witness to Amanda's sentiment.

As seen in Figure 10.2, agreement with the statement "I would work harder and for longer hours if the job demanded it" is strongly related to how often direct reports perceive their leaders "make it a point to let people know they have confidence in their abilities." Not surprisingly, the results (shape of the curve) are nearly identical when measuring how productive people feel in their jobs with how often leaders let them know they have confidence in their abilities.

Neither Amanda nor Connie needed anyone's permission to get started paying attention to the good work of others and letting them know that this mattered. Nor do you. Novelist and nonfiction author

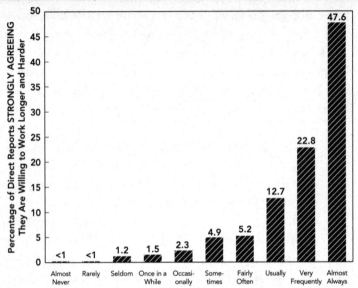

Figure 10.2 Motivation increases when leaders express their confidence in people's abilities.

Anne Lamott offers this captivating story about how to get started. Although her story is about writing, we think the lesson applies to leadership:

> Thirty years ago, my older brother, who was ten years old at the time, was trying to get a report written on birds that he'd had three months to write, which was due the next day. We were out at our family cabin in Bolinas, and he was at the kitchen table close to tears, surrounded by binder paper and pencils and unopened books on birds, immobilized by the hugeness of the task ahead. Then my father sat down beside him, put his arm around my brother's shoulder, and said, "Bird by bird, buddy. Just take it bird by bird."[8]

The possibilities for encouraging the heart seem endless. Author and educator Bob Nelson documents this in his books with *1,001 Ways to Reward Employees*, *1,001 Ways to Energize Employees*, and *1,001 Ways to Engage Employees.*[9] All you have to do is get started. Pick one of Nelson's 3,003 ways—or any of the hundred ways we offer in Chapter 12.

Leaders Go First

Setting the example inevitably involves going first and, by your actions, demonstrating to others what you believe is essential. In addition, when you go first, you send a powerful signal about what behaviors, actions, and decisions you expect of everyone around you. Here are several different applications of this principle.

Sonya Lopes is the school reform coordinator at a public middle school in northern California. She also manages the organization development and change process in the school. Sonya says, "I'm an advisor-critic-listener-reflective partner-confidante to the principal." Sonya decided that she didn't want opportunities for fun at work to pass her by and she started by simply displaying the word *Fun!* in many visible places around the school. She put it on a sign outside the principal's door so she could see it whenever she walked out. She put it in his daily planner as a bookmark. "It helped me," she said, "become more proactive in the search for 'fun' opportunities." For example, one week, she had people turn in their "regular old staff meeting questionnaire" by making the completed survey into paper airplanes and flying them to her. Sonya realized that "for the first time ever, *everyone* turned in their questionnaire!"

Sonya started talking to everyone about having more fun at work. She purchased a box of apple cinnamon muffin mix and made eight huge muffins. In staff mailboxes Sonya left a personalized positive note about why she was leaving the muffins along with a tea bag for them to brew. Inspired by Sonya's spirit of uplifting hearts, the PTA created a livelier school environment during Teacher Appreciation Week. They even decorated the staff bathrooms with tables, potpourri, and colorful wall hangings—everywhere you looked, there was color, color, color. "The teachers," Sonya reported, "talked about it for *days*." Sonya received smiles, hugs, and notes for her actions. "Simply mentioning that fun would be on the agenda at a retreat I was organizing created an exciting buzz and built teachers' curiosity about what we would be doing," she found. Sonya saw the school environment change. Most importantly, Sonya learned a lesson that everyone who begins this journey learns: "Encouraging the heart of others encouraged *my* heart. I was uplifted as I went around smiling, making eye contact with people, and saying their names! I felt *excited* while making muffins and attaching notes to them as spirit lifters for teachers."

Mary McHugo, a high-tech company's corporate counsel, had a similar experience to Sonya's when she decided to "live with" encouraging the heart. Mary took this leadership practice beyond her workplace and incorporated encouraging the heart at home, in her graduate school program, and even with strangers:

> I complimented the person if I saw someone wearing a sweater that I found particularly attractive, rather than admiring it in silence. Sometimes, they were surprised, but more often they were pleased. When I returned from a trip to Alaska, I picked out a few culinary items from the region (candies, fruit, etc.) to set out in the break room on my first day back in the office and share with my colleagues. While leafing through a mail-order catalog, I saw a silver pin depicting three girls. The artist who designed and made the pin named it "The Three Sisters." I ordered three pins and gave one each to my two sisters, and I kept one. It had been quite a while since we had given the other a gift "just because."

In the process of making encouraging the heart part of her lifestyle, Mary also tried hard to listen more actively to her daughter, Katie. She heard in one conversation that her daughter wished for more time with her mom. So, Mary responded by offering weekly mom-and-daughter outings for coffee and hot chocolate. "Several weeks later," she told us, "Katie asked me why I had started doing this. I told her I had been listening to her lament about not being able to spend enough time with me and that I thought this would be a nice way to let her know what a good job she was doing and how proud I was of her. Was this okay with her? She was thrilled. I am unsure which was more meaningful for Katie: our weekly chats at Starbucks or that I heard what she was asking for."

This brief sampling of ways leaders encourage the heart demonstrates that most of what you do are the little things. And that's the point. It doesn't take a grand plan to begin to set an example for encouraging the heart. It doesn't take a huge budget, psychotherapy, or the boss's permission. The most critical thing in all these examples is that the leaders took the initiative. Encouraging the heart became a priority.

One more consideration in setting an example is acknowledging that while people associate recognition with feeling valued, most people are not entirely comfortable with being recognized themselves.[10] Remember, you need to be a role model. If you are not gracefully accepting a compliment, you may make people nervous and anxious about giving them. They'll be worried that their intentions will be misinterpreted, will be seen as kissing up, will trigger jealousy, or will create embarrassment.

When someone compliments you, they are sharing their feelings that you did something that impacted them. It doesn't matter if you completely agree or disagree with what they are saying or think the actions weren't a "big deal" on your part. Just accept this gift, as you would hope they would do the same, and say, "Thank you, that really makes my day," or "I am happy to know that you feel that way," or "I appreciate your taking the time to let me know about that." Don't negate their sentiments by making jokes, discounting the efforts, or bypassing the action. If the credit belongs to someone else, obviously, redirect the compliment by suggesting they share the recognition directly with the correct person.[11]

Setting the example for encouraging the heart begins by permitting yourself to do so. It begins with putting it in your daily planner. It starts with posting a sign by your door, cubicle, or even in the background of your video chats. It begins when you talk to everyone about it. It starts when you turn a routine task into something fun. It begins by giving to others first. It starts when you get personally involved. When leaders get personally involved in encouraging the heart, the results are always the same: the receiver and the giver both feel uplifted.

REFLECT ON
SETTING THE EXAMPLE

Ask Yourself:

1. What do I see when I look in the mirror at work? Is it a smiling, friendly face? Or a severe and stern face?
2. How does my behavior reflect the culture or environment in my workplace?
3. What have I consciously done recently to send a signal to people that encouraging the heart is essential?
4. What would happen if I made encouraging the heart part of my daily habits? What can I do to remind myself of the importance of encouragement?
5. How personally involved am I in the recognition and celebrations that now go on in this organization?
6. What are the unique ways that I demonstrate my appreciation of others?
7. Who is the most credible person in my workplace? What do they do that brings them credibility? How can I incorporate these attributes into my behaviors?

PART THREE

CHAPTER 11

Leadership Is an Affair of the Heart

The best and most beautiful things in the world cannot be seen or even touched—they must be felt with the heart.

—*HELEN KELLER*
The Story of My Life

THE OLYMPICS PROVIDE an exemplary example of the power of encouragement. Thousands of people scream athletes' names. Crowds cheer the athletes along. People jump up and down as the athletes cross the finish line or complete their routines. People clap in unison. They shout go, go, go! You can do it! Vamos! Allez, allez, allez. All of this is to encourage the players to do their best and show their appreciation for medal-winning performances. After events, flags are waved proudly. There are tears of joy, as well as tears of sadness at the end. There are embraces, hugs, and high fives. Emotions are all on full display for the world to see, hear, and feel. If you want to get pumped up to encourage the heart, watch a video clip of a gold medal event.

Okay, this is the Olympics, an event happening once every two or four years, and maybe some of this wouldn't be appropriate for your organization.

It is, however, living proof that human beings have the innate capacity to show joy, appreciation, exuberance, and awe. Why not bring a little bit of these feelings and expressions to work? Why not generate these opportunities, allowing people to let out an occasional whoop or smack a high five? Why not create a space where people can express their joy over a hard-earned success and strengthen community and togetherness?

When you hear sportscasters talk about athletes who dig deep and make that extra effort to win the match, the meet, or the medal, they say, "They had a lot of heart." When you read news stories about someone who dedicated themselves to something challenging, observers often report, "It took a lot of heart." When you hear a story about someone who kept going despite all the odds, you say, "A lot of people would have given up. They really had to put their heart into it to keep on going." But you rarely, if ever, hear that said about managers. Why is that?

There's a prevailing myth that managers are supposed to divorce their emotions from the situation and approach things purely rationally. Whenever you hear someone say, "It's not personal; it's just business," you already know they have detached themselves from whatever they might be feeling. The trouble with this kind of advice is that it's completely misguided. Research that we have cited extensively in this book shows that the highest-performing organizations have the most open and caring leaders. The best leaders show affection toward others and want others to be more open with them. They are more optimistic, positive, passionate, loving, compassionate, grateful, and encouraging than their lower-performing counterparts.

The truth is that *leadership is an affair of the heart*. It takes a lot of heart to be exemplary at leading. There are no Olympic winners without heart, nor is there much integrity and honor without heart. There's no commitment and conviction without heart. There's no hope and faith without heart. There's no trust and support without heart. There's no persistence and courage without heart. There's no learning and risk-taking without heart. Nothing important and meaningful ever gets done without heart. Exemplary leaders excel at improving performance by paying great attention to the human heart.

Leading with Heart

Parker Palmer, author, educator, and activist, and founder of the Center for Courage and Renewal, has observed:

> The power of authentic leadership. . .is found not in external arrangements but in the human heart. Authentic leaders in every setting—from families to nation-states—aim at liberating the heart, their own and others', so that its power can liberate the world.[1]

Nothing external will save any of us from the threats facing our planet, organizations, communities, and ourselves. Not governments, companies, technologies, or heroes on white horses. But imagine what can be done when people experience the power of the human heart. You have the power to make a meaningful contribution to positive change when you lead with your heart.

Gary Burnison, CEO of Korn Ferry, notes that people don't usually think about love and leadership in the same sentence, and yet he contends:

> [L]eadership always begins with our hearts. Face it: leaders need others—we need others. We seek to establish a connection—with authenticity and empathy. That remains the most powerful way to change minds and win hearts.
>
> Affirming others is more than the generic "good job" or even "I'm proud of you." Affirmation is the heartfelt "I believe in you."
>
> When people are told, "We couldn't have done this without you," the message delivered is, "You are loved."[2]

These poetic and powerful perspectives from Parker and Gary are spot on. Remember what we said at the beginning of our discussion of encouraging the heart: leadership is a relationship, and the quality of that relationship matters most. When the quality of your relationship—your connection—with others is one of caring, authenticity, empathy, and affirmation, people will want to put forth more effort, stick around through rough times, work more collaboratively with others, express more pride in the place they work, and feel that their work has more meaning and purpose.

Building and sustaining that kind of relationship takes a lot of heart. It takes heart to be open about deeply held beliefs, to have faith in the capacity of others, to get close and personal with people, to empathize and listen with big ears, to tell stories publicly, to show joy and appreciation, to celebrate when others succeed, and to make yourself vulnerable by being the first to set the example.

That's why encouraging the heart is the most personal of the leadership practices. Affirming others and showing your appreciation requires you to make other people the center of your attention and ensure that they know you feel they're important. You can't do that from a distance. You have to get personal.

You also have to answer a very important question, perhaps the most important question any leader has to answer: How much do I care about the people I lead?

Our hunch is that you care a lot. You probably wouldn't be reading this book if you didn't. However, the question must still be confronted daily. It's an ongoing process. When you care deeply, the essentials we have described are no longer tools, techniques, or strategies—but genuine expressions of your caring. When those around you perceive you as caring little, your actions will be seen as insincere, nothing more than gimmicks, and you're considered a phony, perhaps even a hypocrite.

Showing you care about the people you lead makes them feel you have their best interests at heart. Research indicates that when people feel that others care about them, they work harder. But when they feel they're being treated uncaringly or rudely at work, they respond by deliberately decreasing their effort or lowering the quality of their work.[3] Our data reveals that the extent to which direct reports feel their leader has "the best interests of other people at work" relates directly to their level of team spirit and pride. It's also directly related to how favorably they evaluate their leader's effectiveness and the likelihood that they would recommend that individual to a colleague as a good leader.

As we've maintained throughout this book, demonstrating that you care about others isn't rocket science. For example, Valarie Chaplin, responsible for leadership development at a large public Canadian university, found that most faculty and staff just desired simple gestures, showing that she and others cared about what and how they were doing. This often took the form of a personal note or email, a comment during a meeting or in the hallways outside a classroom, or just a quick stop by their office. "What they want to know is that I value them," Valarie said. "They want to hear from me how I believe they are doing great work and that neither they nor their contributions are being taken for granted. In my experience, this doesn't require grand, over-the-top actions." Indeed, the size of the gesture is seldom critical; it is very simply that you noticed their contribution.

Our data backs up Valarie's experience. It shows a statistically significant correlation between how much their direct reports feel valued and how often their leader "praises people for a job well done." The research shows that people who believe they are cared about, in turn, care more about their work and are more likely to want to continue working with their leader.[4]

In essence, it's all about showing respect for others. Making other people the center of your attention tells them you feel they matter, that you regard what they say as important, and you value their ideas and perspectives. Our research, and practically everyone else's on leadership, clearly shows that performance is significantly better when leaders treat people with dignity and respect, listen to them, support them, recognize them, make them feel important, build their skills, and show confidence in them.

In a large-scale study of leader communication in the workplace, researchers found that "recognition from leaders that conveys to employees an acknowledgment for their specific accomplishments not only contributes to better outcomes for employees but also fosters a culture in which employees respect each other's contributions. This respectful, supportive workplace culture, in turn, contributes to positive job outcomes for employees."[5] It's a virtuous circle. When organizational leaders show they care about and respect their employees, employees do the same with their colleagues. The well-being and performance of everyone improve.

The Encouraging Leader's Quest

Of course, none of this comes easily. It takes a lot of effort to make people feel valued, encouraged, confident, cared for, and capable of doing more than they thought possible. You have to work hard to become an exemplary leader who cares.

But here's the good news. Doing so has nothing to do with your personality, genetic disposition, the family you were born into, the neighborhood you came from, the school you attended, how old you are, or any other demographic variable. Nor does it depend on your position, function, discipline, industry, company size, years of work experience, or tenure. It's all about how you behave.

If it's your behavior that matters, then specific skills are needed. When skills are involved, these can be learned, developed, and honed so you can perform them better than you do now. Of course, only if you want to. Do you? We know from our research that if you put the time and effort into learning (including good coaching and practice), you can become an even more effective leader.[6]

Leadership development is self-development. The instrument of leadership is the self, and mastery of the art of leadership comes from mastery of the self. Self-development is not about stuffing in a whole bunch of new information or trying out the latest technique. It's about leading out of what is already in your soul. It's about liberating the leader within you. It's about setting yourself free.

The quest for leadership is first an inner quest to discover who you are. Learning to lead is about discovering what *you* value. About what inspires *you*. About what challenges *you*. About what gives *you* power and competence. About what encourages *you*. When you discover these things about yourself, you'll know what it takes to lead those qualities out of others.

Discovering who you are is something every artist understands, and they know it is not a matter of technique. It's a matter of time and searching—soul searching. When attending a painter and printmaker's retrospective exhibition with an artist friend, he described three periods in an artist's life. In the first, he explained, "We paint exterior landscapes. In the second, we paint interior landscapes. In the third period, we paint ourselves, which is when we begin to have our own unique style." This was an insightful art appreciation lesson—and it applies equally to appreciation of the art of leadership.

When you first learn to lead, you paint (imitate) what you see outside of yourself, the exterior landscape. You read biographies and autobiographies and watch documentaries about famous leaders. You read trade books by experienced executives and dedicated scholars. You attend speeches given by decorated military officers. You buy tapes of motivational speakers, and you participate in classes, seminars, workshops, and training programs with skilled facilitators.

In this essential period, you do all this to master the fundamentals, the tools, and the techniques. Unsurprisingly, you are often clumsy at first, failing more than succeeding, but soon, you can give a speech with ease, conduct a meeting with grace, and praise an employee with style. An aspiring leader can no more skip the fundamentals than can an aspiring painter.

Then it happens. Somewhere along the way, you notice how that last speech sounded mechanical and rote, how that last meeting was a boring routine, and how that last encounter felt terribly sad and empty. You awaken to the frightening thought that the words aren't yours, that the vocabulary is someone else's, that the technique is right out of the text but not straight from the heart.

This is a terrifying moment. Having invested so much time and energy in learning to do all the right things, you suddenly see that they no longer serve you well. They seem hollow, and you feel like an imposter. You stare into your inner landscape's darkness and wonder what lies there.

For aspiring leaders, this awakening initiates a period of intense exploration. In this second period, you mix and test new ingredients and experiment with different techniques. You go beyond training, copying what the masters do, and taking the advice of others. Stay the course, because it's well worth the price of exhausting experimentation and sometimes painful suffering when you reach the third period. From all those abstract strokes on the canvas emerges an expression of self that is yours alone.

Most leadership development is still at stage one. It's mostly about painting exterior landscapes, copying other people's styles, and mimicking great leaders. We hope to encourage you to move beyond stage one and explore your inner territory so that you can find your own style, your unique and authentic voice.

We know you can learn to lead. Leadership is not limited or bounded by function, position, or place. Don't confuse leadership with tools and techniques or structures and systems. They're not what earns you the respect and commitment of your constituents. Ultimately, what earns you respect is whether you are what you say you are and whether what you are embodies what others want to become. When people feel their leaders care about them, they willingly enlist in tackling the unknown.

Now that you've reached the end of the book, you should have heaps of ideas about what you can and need to do. As St. Ignatius, the Spanish priest and theologian who founded the Jesuit order, wisely said, "To know, and not to do, is not to know." With that in mind, do something. If you're still wondering where to begin, we've shared more than 100 specific actions you can take in the next chapter. Get started doing.

CHAPTER 12

101 Ways to Encourage the Heart

ENCOURAGEMENT COMES IN packages of all kinds. We've seen it done quietly with a thank you, a story, and a smile, and we've been part of grand Academy Awards–style productions. Your imagination is the only limit.

This chapter provides some ideas to get you started. Most are collected examples of what we've observed and what others have contributed to us. Use what we list here to stimulate your creativity. Adapt the ideas to your situation; combine them or use them singularly.

We've categorized the ideas under the seven essentials so you can focus on the areas you need to work on most. However, many of these actions include more than one essential element.

Most importantly, have fun with this. These activities are designed to facilitate your learning; learning to do a better job of encouraging the heart should be a joyous process.

The First Essential: Set Clear Standards

1. Take time to clarify the values or "operating principles" essential for you and your team to live by. Write down your answer to this question: "What values do I believe should guide my daily decisions and actions and those of the people with whom I work and interact?" We sometimes refer to this as the "credo memo" exercise. It's like a note you send to your colleagues before you take off for an extended sabbatical, telling them that while you're not around, these are the principles you want them to use to govern their actions and decisions.

2. Ask your associates—with whom you work regularly—to prepare their own credo memo.

3. Keep current. If you've already done the exercise in item one, get the piece of paper on which you wrote your values and ask yourself, "To what extent do these *still* represent the values that I believe should guide our daily decisions and actions? Is there anything I want to add? Anything I want to delete? Any priorities I want to change?"

4. Post your values statement conspicuously so you'll regularly be reminded of your principles. Put it on your bulletin board in your office or workstation; make it a Star Wars–style screen saver; attach it to your computer as a yellow sticky note. Martin Luther nailed his beliefs on the cathedral door centuries ago, and it started quite a movement! Why not you?

5. Make the topic of one of your next team meetings "Our Values." Ask everyone to state aloud what they believe in. Listen and observe. What values does everyone seem to share in common? What values seem unique to some individuals? Are there any significant values conflicts? Talk about how you can honor

individual values yet have shared values that govern your collective behavior as a team. Post collective values in visible places all around your workplace common areas.

6. If your organization has a corporate creed or some published statement of values, compare it to your and your team's credos. To what extent are they compatible? To what extent are there some conflicts? How good is the fit between organizational and personal values? What needs to be changed? What needs recommitment?

7. Make sure people get regular, specific feedback. Remember what we learned from the research: the combination of feedback and goals is encouraging in itself. When people know where they're headed and how far they've gone, they feel better, are physically healthier, and achieve higher performance. Make sure that people get regular feedback on their progress toward goals. It might even come from you: "Hey, we've reached a project milestone. Well done. Let's celebrate!"

8. Better yet, create ways for people to monitor themselves so they know how much progress they've made. The software we're using to write this book enables us at any instant to compute how many pages, words, paragraphs, lines, and characters we've written. We know what our contract requires regarding the number of pages and the deadlines. We're entirely self-monitoring. That sure feels better than getting bugged by the editor daily, asking, "What progress are you making? How are you doing?"

9. The next time—and every time—you recognize an individual or a group for doing the right thing or doing things right, make sure to refer to the standard they exemplify. Announce it at the beginning of your recognition, and repeat it at the end. Say something like, "One of the things we stand for around here is knock-your-socks-off service to our customers. Just yesterday, Bev did something to exemplify that value. Let me tell you about it. . . .And remember, just as Bev did, let's knock their socks off every time!"

10. If your company gives bonuses, start looking for ways to link some portion of the bonus to how people are meeting or exceeding the cherished values of the organization. When it's time to hand out the checks, attach a short note mentioning the actions that exemplified the values. At one company we've worked with, 33 percent of the bonus-eligible managers' incentive pay is directly linked to how much they've lived out the values. Their ratings come from their direct reports. Now, that's putting your money where your mouth is.

11. Participate in a personal retreat or an offsite with your team to explore meaning and purpose in life and work.

12. Think of someone you admire who exemplifies living a principle-centered life. Interview that person and find out how they discovered their values.

13. Invent or select symbolic ways of visibly marking people's progress, as the scouts, the military, and many professional organizations do. Pins, ribbons, badges, patches, medals, certificates, and the like that signify "You made it to the next level" send meaningful messages to the receivers and their friends, families, and colleagues.

The Second Essential: Expect the Best

14. Remember the principle of the self-fulfilling prophecy: people tend to act consistently with your expectations of them. The Pygmalion effect also applies to you, so be positive and optimistic about your ability to lead and the achievements of the people around you. How? Surround yourself with positive people who can remind you of your strengths and abilities.

15. Practice smiling. This is not a joke. Smiling and laughing release naturally occurring chemicals in people's bodies that fight off depression and uplift their moods. Try it.

16. Ask yourself: "Do I honestly believe everyone on my team can achieve our goals and live by the values we've agreed upon?" If your answer is yes, make sure that you communicate this to them verbally and nonverbally. If your answer is no, figure out what you can do to change your answer to yes. Make those changes. You can do it.

17. The next time you talk to one of your constituents about a difficulty they are having with a project, make sure that sometime during the conversation, you say, "I know you can do it," or words to that effect. And you better mean it.

18. Assign people to essential tasks that aren't part of their defined job. Let them know you have assigned them these unusual jobs because you strongly believe in them—that you believe they can excel at them. Make a binding commitment to supply them with the training, resources, authority, and coaching they need to be successful.

19. Buy a few inspirational posters and put them on the walls of your facility. If you don't like the ones in the catalogs, then add posters of images that symbolize the spirit you'd like to promote in your workplace. Through these or other means, find some way to make your positive expectations visible.

20. Walk around your facility and examine the images on the walls. Are they images that communicate positive messages or negative ones? Analyze your company's annual report, executive speeches (including your own!), the company newsletter, and other forms of corporate communication. Are the messages positive or negative? Do whatever you can to change the messages to positive ones.

21. Each time you coach or train people to acquire new knowledge or a new skill, make sure you say that you know this skill can be acquired. Tell them they can learn it. Even if you think this is obvious, say it out loud anyway. It's essential to send the message to your learners. Of course, you've got to believe it yourself, so if in reality you don't think a particular skill can be learned and that it's innate instead, please do everyone a favor and don't accept an assignment to teach it.

The Third Essential: Pay Attention

22. If you are co-located with your team, leave your desk or workstation for fifteen minutes daily to learn more about them. Who are they? What are their needs and aspirations? What do they need to find greater joy in their work?

23. If you're a virtual company and don't have the opportunity to visit everyone you work with, ask people to describe their workspace in detail. Ask them probing questions about what's on their desks, what's on the walls, and so on. When on video calls, pay particular attention to what you can see displayed around them. Tell them you're trying to get a feel for their space like you do with the people down the hall whose space you do see.

24. Note the kinds of "gifts" or recognition people appreciate (or don't appreciate). Remember, for some people, all that glitters is not gold!

25. Start a file of recognition ideas on your computer or in a journal that you can carry in your briefcase, purse, or pocket. Record the ideas that come to you for recognizing and rewarding individual contributions and celebrating team accomplishments. Please keep your eyes and ears open for those moments we all encounter when we experience or witness particularly

effective types of recognition you could use. You might also pick up some ideas from television dramas, movies, or books. A journal where you can jot these down becomes a tool for remembering good ideas and focusing your search for new ways to encourage the heart.

26. Don't wait for a ceremony as a reason to recognize someone. If you notice something that deserves immediate recognition, go up and say, "I was just noticing how you handled that customer complaint. How you listened actively and responded was a real model of what we're looking for. What you've done is an example to everyone. Thank you." If you happen to be carrying around a few extra coupons for a free drink at the local coffee or juice shop, here's an opportunity to give one out.

27. Record the birthdays of your critical constituents on your computer, tablet, or paper calendar. Also, write down their anniversary dates of joining the organization. Send a note or visit on those dates.

28. Put yourself in another person's shoes for a while. Volunteer to do someone else's job. People will appreciate your efforts, and you'll better understand what your colleagues do.

29. Make a short list of people performing their work above stated expectations and how they best embody the team's values and priorities. Jot down at least three ways to recognize these people and show your appreciation over the next couple of weeks

30. Imagine someone following you with a video camera and filming your daily wanderings. Now imagine that you are watching the video. What behavioral signals are you sending? Are they communicating that you're looking for people doing things right and doing the right things? What specific behaviors can you adopt that communicate *I'm here to find all the positive examples I can*?

31. The next time you watch an awards ceremony like the Grammys or Oscars, pay particular attention to which acceptance speeches you like, which you don't like, and why. Incorporate the best of these ideas into your acts of recognition.

32. The next time you listen to someone talk about themselves, their work, and what's important, listen with your "eyes and heart," not just your ears and brain. What do you notice when listening with your eyes and heart that you don't when listening with your ears and brain?

33. At your next team meeting, disclose something about yourself that others don't know. We're not talking about deep, dark secrets here, just something that enables others to get to know you better. For example, how many siblings you have, what it was like growing up in your house, your first memory of working in the organization, your favorite screw-up of all time, anything that makes you more open to others. Encourage the same in them. Remember, openness leads to trust, which is essential to your credibility. Try practicing more transparency.

34. Ask your colleagues for feedback about your performance, particularly about how you are doing in encouraging the heart. The ground rules are that you can only ask questions for clarification and only respond by saying thank you.

The Fourth Essential: Personalize Recognition

35. Think back to when someone meaningfully and memorably encouraged your heart. What did they do to make it memorable for you? How did they personalize it for you? Please make note of the lessons you learned and apply them.

36. Tell people in your organization your own "most meaningful recognition story." Ask them to tell theirs. What are the common experiences and lessons?

37. Talk with friends outside of work. Ask them to tell you stories about receiving recognition that particularly moved or affected them. Sometimes, informal talks can lead to great ideas because you can share and understand people's inner experiences and how they are affected by having their efforts acknowledged.

38. As they do at many airlines, give your customers, vendors, and other employees coupons to award to people who do something exceptional. You can also make the coupons redeemable for prizes, but it's not the size of the award that matters; it's the signal you send that says, "I appreciate you."

39. Make every effort to personalize every recognition so the recipient feels uniquely appreciated. For the avid cyclist in your office, for instance, recognize them with a small plastic model of a bike for the desktop; attach a note that says, "For a quick spin around the block when you're working late."

40. Send champagne or sparkling cider and flowers to the family of your next Super Person of the Month.

41. Whenever you plan an act of recognition, ask yourself, "What can I do to ensure this is special, memorable, and unique for this person?"

42. When presenting a gift at a recognition ceremony, ask yourself, "How do I know this is something the individual would appreciate?"

43. Create symbols for certain kinds of recognition in your organization. We have often used a zebra. It's incredible how many zebra T-shirts, cups, mugs, pencils, pins, cards, and what-have-you there are! Be creative in devising your rewards; have some fun with them.

44. Enlist the help of someone close to the person you intend to recognize. Ask that person what this individual likes and what would make the recognition memorable.

45. Publish captioned photos or the names of people you want to recognize in a company newsletter, annual report, social media platform, or department handout. If there's room, include a brief story describing the person's exceptional contribution.

46. Create your organization's Hall of Fame: an area for small plaques and handwritten notes recognizing all the people who've done extraordinary things. If you work in a virtual environment, consider setting up a Slack or Teams channel to recognize noteworthy achievements.

47. Contribute to an employee's favorite charity and announce it at a company party or department get-together.

48. Say thank you personally every time you appreciate something someone does, anywhere and anytime. It's good practice and good manners.

49. When complimenting an individual or a team, be specific about what they did that was laudable. Give enough details and examples to provide a context for your appreciation. Describe their actions' impact on you, the team, customers, or others.

The Fifth Essential: Tell the Story

50. You will likely recognize an individual or group in the next few days. Whatever else you do, tell the story of what was done in as much detail as possible. If possible, figure out a way to reenact the incident.

51. Tell someone the story of your most meaningful recognition at one of your next virtual or in-person meetings. Explain you're doing it to encourage them to do the same at a meeting.

52. Devote an entire team meeting to having each person tell the story of their most meaningful recognition. Set aside some time at meetings to allow people to brag about something.

53. Dedicate another team meeting solely to telling stories on the theme of "I heard something good about you" concerning *colleagues* they work with.

54. Never pass up any opportunity to publicly relate true stories about how people in your organization have gone above and beyond the call of duty. Hallways, elevators, cafeterias, and meeting rooms are all acceptable venues for telling a good story.

55. When you present a public recognition, try to do it where the action occurred. If that's not feasible, at least describe the scene to people so they can picture it in their minds. All good stories create a sense of place.

56. Don't forget voicemail, email, and social media; these are good media for telling stories. Although people tend to want shorter stories in these formats, they're still helpful ways to disseminate good news. One of our colleagues starts the day at his organization by leaving a recorded message for everyone that tells at least one story of catching someone doing something right.

57. Keep a journal. Record the critical incidents of the day in as much detail as possible. Capture as many examples of outstanding and commendable performance as you can. The practice of observing and recording will build your storytelling skills.

58. Ask a professional storyteller—yes, they exist—to participate in one of your leadership seminars and teach everyone some tips

for good storytelling. You can also find some examples online. And if you're serious about learning storytelling, here's a link to a course from the Kahn Academy entitled "Pixar in a Box": https://www.khanacademy.org/computing/pixar.

59. At dinner every night, don't just talk about your day; tell a story about it. Describe the rich details of place, people, and feelings. Use your home as a practice stage.

60. Interview an actor who does improvisational theater. Ask them to share some ways of taking a simple idea from the audience and turning it into a story.

The Sixth Essential: Celebrate Together

61. Every celebration has a potential dual purpose. One is to offer social support, something we know makes people happier, healthier, and better-performing. The other is to honor an individual, group, or entire organization for upholding a cherished standard. While we celebrate Independence Day with fireworks, food, drink, and fun, we also celebrate the value of freedom and those who have dedicated their lives to keeping us free. Organizational celebrations have this same function. Ask yourself about the fundamental principles being honored and how everyone will have fun.

62. Visit a party store in your neighborhood. You can pick up countless ideas for making something more festive.

63. Visit an organization you know with a reputation for being a fun workplace. Find out what makes them so inventive when it comes to celebration.

64. At a wedding or other celebratory event, note what you like or what inspires you about the event. See if you can incorporate these ideas into your plans to encourage the heart.

65. Start an informal celebration task force if your organization doesn't celebrate much. It probably has to be a skunk-works operation since, with a few notable exceptions, CEOs don't tend to sponsor these kinds of projects. Make it your job to liven up the place, borrowing from others' inventiveness and creating your own fun and games at work.

66. Put up a "bragging board" in your workspace where you can post notes of appreciation from customers, vendors, and colleagues. Invite everyone to contribute notes and pictures of themselves and others.

67. End each of your team meetings with a round of public praising.

68. During change and transition, get people together to talk about how they're feeling and doing. Social support is critical at these times, so schedule regular opportunities for people to lean on each other. If the situation is particularly intense, getting an outside facilitator to work with your group might be helpful.

69. Be sure to mark particularly significant transitions with special celebrations—things like the anniversary of the organization's founding, a merger or acquisition, the launch of a new product, and so on.

70. Give every celebration a theme, and include a surprise at some point during the evening.

71. Formal events are essential, but informal ones are likely more frequent and accessible. Organize informal ways to unite eople: special lunches, picnics, noontime athletic events (volleyball, shooting baskets, softball games, etc.), and anything that

promotes camaraderie and interpersonal support. Consider hosting fun lunches, watch parties, games, or other events over Zoom in a virtual workplace.

72. When organizing a celebration, ensure everyone knows the reason for the celebration.

73. Get people involved in planning celebrations. Don't try to do it all yourself. Joint planning offers social support, makes people laugh together, and generates more creativity than if one person handles everything.

74. Put a microwave near your office door. At about 3:00 p.m. each day, cook some popcorn. Invite folks to take a break and join you for a brief discussion about their day. If popcorn isn't your thing, how about an ice cream vending machine or fruit basket?

75. Always keep a few party favors handy. You never know when you might want to throw a spontaneous celebration when an employee announces a wedding, birth, or other personal achievement. You can also be "spontaneous" virtually by emailing or texting a surprise note to people about the good news. Of course, you can include a fun emoji or GIF that brings a smile to people's faces. And use those reaction images on Zoom when you want to show your appreciation.

76. Print up note cards that say at the top, "I heard something good about you. . ." Leave enough blank space for people to write a personalized note to a coworker describing the particular situation for which they're being recognized. Use them yourself to recognize your employees, but give every employee a stack of these cards to hand out and encourage them to recognize one another. Provide a bulletin board in a conspicuous place where people who've received cards can display them.

77. Recognize your staff with a simple pin that says, "Caught caring!" In an environment where people often can't say thank you, these pins mean much to staff members. They represent tangible evidence that someone recognizes how much they give.

78. Plan festive celebrations for even the smaller milestones that your team reaches. Don't wait until the whole project is completed before you celebrate. Immediate acknowledgment keeps energy and enthusiasm high.

79. Set aside one day each year as a special organization-wide celebration, much like Independence Day or Mardi Gras.

80. At one of your next meetings, make the only agenda item to discuss how people feel about working in the organization.

81. Take care of your own needs for support. To find out what your support network looks like, in the center of a piece of paper, draw a circle about the size of a half-dollar. Write your name in it. Draw smaller circles around the big one to represent people you can turn to for personal support; draw some of them nearer to the center and some farther away. Think about your closest relationships and jot down their names in the circles nearest your name. Work quickly, writing in names as they pop into your mind. Next, in the circles farther out from the center, name people you can lean on, but not necessarily ones in whom you can confide your troubles. Take a moment to study what you've done. Who can you count on? Does the sketch include people from all areas of your life? Ask yourself how much support you feel from each of them. Does anything need to change?

The Seventh Essential: Set the Example

82. Do a DWYSYWD audit. Take a sheet of paper and draw a line down the middle. On the left-hand side, record your values, which are the principles by which you say you want to lead your organization. On the right-hand side, record your actions: what you do regularly to live out each of your values. Of course, the only way to get any value from this exercise is to be entirely

transparent. Leave the space blank if you don't see yourself doing anything to live out a value. If you think your behaviors contradict the values you espouse, write down that admission. Grade yourself on how you're doing. Do your values and actions line up? Where are you strong? Where do you have opportunities for improvement? Plan to align values and actions better.

83. Conduct a DWWSWWD audit (recall Chapter 10). Use the same process you used in number 82 above, and assess how well people are living up to the values the group says they share.

84. Become more visible. You're supposed to set the example, and people must see you doing what you say.

85. Get personally involved in as many recognition events and celebrations, in person and virtual, as possible. If you don't attend staff celebrations, you're sending the message that you're not interested. That lack of interest will be mirrored back to you.

86. Identify those experiences in your life that truly inspire you, and then bring this inspiration into your conversations with employees.

87. Write and deliver at least three thank-you notes every day. We've never heard anyone complain about being thanked too much, but we've all heard lots of complaints about being thanked too little!

88. Look around for someone you know or have heard about who is much better at encouraging the heart than you are. Ask for their advice and some coaching.

89. Ask a colleague for feedback on how you are encouraging the heart and their advice about how you could improve.

90. Every time you start a meeting, make sure to affirm your commitment to the values you all share. The frequent repetition of a commitment starts you moving in that direction. The more people you tell, and the more often you say it, the harder it is to back out.

91. Post your values where you and others can see them.

92. Identify a positive role model for each of the seven essentials of encouraging the heart. Make sure you can envision someone who does each of these practices well.

93. Practice the seven essentials regularly and extensively. If possible, sessions should be conducted with a coach or trusted colleague present so that you can receive feedback on your progress.

94. Give yourself some credit for practicing and applying the seven essentials. Find a way to reward yourself for doing what you say.

95. Create a recognition reminder notice, screen saver, or other device to make visible how you can encourage the heart.

96. Think of someone in your department or organization who exemplifies one of your organization's standards. Think of another person who exemplifies another standard. Find a way to make these individuals peer coaches for others.

97. Make sure that others know about your efforts to model encouragement. Tell people stories about how you tried and succeeded or tried and failed. Share the lessons you've learned.

98. Keep a journal of your experiments with encouraging the heart. What works for you? What doesn't? What lessons have you learned? How has this effort changed you as a leader?

99. The next time someone recognizes you, note your thoughts and feelings. (Experience becomes the best teacher, but only if you reflect on it.) Then send that person a thank-you note expressing appreciation for what you learned.

100. Get together with friends and colleagues and generate your own list of ways to encourage the heart. It'd be a great exercise in reinforcing the importance of this practice, and it'd be a whole lot of fun!

Oh, and here's one more for you!

101. Give yourself a standing ovation for having read this book! Your desire to encourage the heart more often and effectively is worth celebrating. We thank you for making a difference.

NOTES

Epigraphs

1. Gostick, A., and Elton, C. *Leading with Gratitude: Eight Business Practices for Extraordinary Business Results*. New York: HarperCollins, 2020.
2. Gallup and Workhuman. *From "Thank You" to Thriving: A Deeper Look at How Recognition Amplifies Wellbeing*. May 18, 2023. Accessed at https://assets.ctfassets.net/hff6luki1ys4/1u0QQs4PbQ2cddH9IwtVSu/4e0df3f622a72621d521d9cc8549e4bf/from-thank-you-to-thriving.pdf.
3. Gardner, J. W. *On Leadership*. New York: Free Press, 1993.
4. Novak, D. *O Great One! A Little Story about the Awesome Power of Recognition*. New York: Penguin Random House, 2016.
5. Joy, H., as quoted in Gostick and Elton, op. cit., p. 101.
6. Hendricks, G., and Ludeman, K. *The Corporate Mystic: A Guidebook for Visionaries with Their Feet on the Ground*. New York: Bantam, 1997.
7. Brady, T., and Nohria, N. "Tom Brady on the Art of Leading Teammates," *Harvard Business Review*, September–October 2024. Accessed at https://hbr.org/2024/09/tom-brady-on-the-art-of-leading-teammates.

Notes

8. Weil, E. *Every Leader Tells a Story*. Fast Company, May 31, 1998. Accessed at https://www.fastcompany.com/34330/every-leader-tells-story.
9. Johnson, W. *Smart Growth: How to Grow Your People to Grow Your Company*. Boston: Harvard Business Review Press, 2022.
10. Hemingway, E. *For Whom the Bell Tolls*. New York: Scribner, 1995.
11. Keller, H. *The Story of My Life*. New York: Dover Publications, Inc., 1996.

Introduction

1. "(You've Gotta Have) Heart," from *Damn Yankees* (1955), music and lyrics by Richard Adler and Jerry Ross.
2. For a detailed description of the research and development of The Five Practices of Exemplary Leadership®, see Kouzes, J. M., and Posner, B. Z., *The Leadership Challenge: How to Make Extraordinary Things Happen in Organizations* (7th ed.). Hoboken, NJ: Wiley, 2023. Encouraging the Heart is one of The Five Practices developed by Kouzes and Posner and is the proprietary name for this leadership practice.
3. The Leadership Practices Inventory (LPI) was developed to assess the frequency with which people engage in The Five Practices of Exemplary Leadership. More than 250,000 individuals annually complete the instrument. We continue to find that the more frequently leaders engage in The Five Practices, the more effective they are, as indicated by various measures of engagement (e.g., commitment, motivation, pride, and performance). The normative LPI database includes nearly 500,000 leaders and more than 4.5 million observers. Almost 1,000 published studies by doctoral students, academics, and practitioners have validated The Five Practices conceptually and as a robust developmental framework. See https://www.leadershipchallenge.com/ for more information about the LPI, including the monograph *Bringing the Rigor of Research to The Art of Leadership: Evidence Behind The Five Practices of Exemplary Leadership*©, Hoboken, NJ: Wiley, 2015.
4. Partridge, E. *Origins: A Short Etymological Dictionary of the Modern English Language*. New York: Macmillan, 1977, p. 120.
5. Anderson, C. A. *Infectious Generosity: The Ultimate Idea Worth Spreading*. New York: Crown Publishing, 2024.

Chapter 1: The Heart of Leadership

1. Stillman, J. "These are the Top 5 Reasons People Are Quitting During the Great Resignation, According to a Massive New Study." January 18, 2022. *Inc.* magazine. Accessed at https://www.inc.com/jessica-stillman/great-resignation-mit-revelio-research.html.

2. Gostick, A., and Elton, C. *Leading with Gratitude: Eight Business Practices for Extraordinary Business Results*. New York: HarperCollins, 2020.

3. Clifton, J., and Harter, J. "It's the Manager: Gallup Finds the Quality of Managers and Team Leaders is the Single Biggest Factor in Your Organization's Long-Term Success." New York: Gallup Press, 2019.

4. Achor, S. *Big Potential: How Transforming the Pursuit of Success Raises Our Achievement, Happiness, and Well-Being*. New York: Currency. 2018.

5. O. C. Tanner Learning Group. "Performance Accelerated: A New Benchmark for Initiative Employee Engagement, Retention, and Results." Accessed at https://edubirdie.com/wp-content/uploads/2024/02/White-Paper-Performance-Accelerated.pdf.

6. O. C. Tanner Learning Group. "10 Ways to Ensure All Your Employees Feel Valued and Appreciated at Work." February 16, 2024. Accessed at https://www.octanner.com/articles/10-ways-to-ensure-all-your-employees-feel-valued-and-appreciated-at-work.

7. O. C. Tanner Learning Group, op. cit.

8. Kepner-Tregoe. *People and Their Jobs: What's Real, What's Rhetoric?* Princeton, NJ: Kepner-Tregoe, 1995, p. 7.

9. Achor, op. cit.

10. We often use the words *purpose* and *meaning* interchangeably. Purpose generally refers to an overarching goal, and in our usage tends to refer to the overall end goal or objective of what one is doing, often collectively as in an organization; meaning is more about how, at the individual level, one derives satisfaction from the work they are doing themselves. Stephen Friedman does an excellent job of helping explain how individuals can get sidetracked in pursuing purpose too early in their careers versus finding meaning in what they are doing (https://hbr.org/2024/04/your-career-doesnt-need-to-have-a-purpose?utm_medium=email&utm_source=newsletter_daily&utm_campaign=mtod_Active&deliveryName=NL_MTOD_20240502).

11. Great Place to Work Institute. "The Power of Purpose in the Workplace." 2023. Accessed at https://www.greatplacetowork.com/resources/reports/the-power-of-purpose-in-the-workplace.

12. Ibid.

13. Unless otherwise indicated, quotes and stories from individuals in this book are from interviews or case studies we collected. We have changed some names to protect their confidentiality and that of their organizations, knowing that many have and will change positions and affiliations over time. It is important to focus on their sentiments, behaviors, and actions rather than their particular positions, titles, functions, industries, and the like.

14. Liu, A. "Making Joy a Priority at Work." *Harvard Business Review,* July 17, 2019.

15. Center for Creative Leadership. "Building Relationship Skills at Work." November 9, 2021. Accessed at https://www.ccl.org/articles/leading-effectively-articles/building-relationship-skills/. Also see Eckert, R., Rudeman, M., Gentry, B., and Stawiski, S. "Through the Looking Glass: How Relationships Shape Managerial Careers." Accessed at https://cclinnovation.org/wp-content/uploads/2020/03/throughthelookingglass.pdf.

16. Telephone interview with Jodi Taylor, former vice president of the Center for Creative Leadership, Colorado Springs, CO, and owner of Taylor Leadership Consulting, July 23, 2024.

17. Goleman, D. *Emotional Intelligence: Why It Can Matter More Than IQ.* New York: Bantam Books, 1995, p. 80.

18. Quoted in Farnham, A. "Are You Smart Enough to Keep Your Job?" *Fortune,* January 15, 1996, p. 36.

19. EY Americas. "Is the Tip of the Spear Where You're Most Comfortable?" February 5, 2022. Accessed at https://www.ey.com/en_us/insights/private-business/is-the-tip-of-the-spear-where-you-re-most-comfortable. Also see Zakl, J. *The War for Kindness: Building Empathy in a Fractured World.* New York: Crown Publishing, 2019, and Lipman, V. "How Important is Empathy to Successful Management?" *Forbes,* February 24, 2018.

20. Dennison, K. "The Importance of Empathy in Leadership: How to Lead with Compassion and Understanding in 2023." February 24, 2023. Accessed at https://www.forbes.com/sites/karadennison/2023/02/24/the-importance-of-empathy-in-leadership-how-to-lead-with-compassion-and-understanding-in-2023/?sh=5d9a49a859e3.

21. Burnison, G. *Love, Hope and Leadership: A Special Edition*. Hoboken, NJ: Wiley, 2024, p. 262.

22. Fulghum, R. *All I Really Need to Know I Learned in Kindergarten: Uncommon Thoughts on Common Things*. New York: Random House, 1989.

23. Kanter, R. M., presentation at Santa Clara University on "The Change Masters," March 13, 1986.

24. Pillay, N. A., Park, G., Kim, Y., and Lee, S. "Thank You for Your Ideas: Gratitude and Team Creativity." *Organizational Behavior and Human Decision Processes* 156 (January 2020): 69–81. Burnison, G. *Love, Hope and Leadership: A Special Edition*. Hoboken, NJ: Wiley, 2024, p. 262.

25. Robson, D. *The Laws of Connection: The Scientific Secrets of Building a Strong Social Network*. New York: Pegasus Books, 2024, pp. 110–111.

26. Emmons, R. and Smith, J. A. "What Gratitude Is and Why It Matters," in Smith, J. A. et al., eds, *The Gratitude Project. How the Science of Thankfulness Can Rewire Our Brains for Resilience, Optimism, and the Greater Good*. Oakland, CA: New Harbinger Publications, 2020, pp. 7–8.

27. Zenger, J., and Folkman, J. "Do You Tell Your Employees You Appreciate Them?" *Harvard Business Review*, September 12, 2022. Accessed at https://hbr.org/2022/09/do-you-tell-your-employees-you-appreciate-them.

28. Lindahl, L. "What Makes a Good Job?" *Personnel* 25 (January 1949): 263–266.

29. Faulconer, E., and Griffith, J. "Do Academic Supervisors Know What Their Employees Want from Work? *Journal of Higher Education Management* 37, no. 2 (2022): 68–79; remodeling, "What Employees Want vs. What their Bosses Think Employees Want, September 27, 2013. Accessed at https://www.remodeling.hw.net/article/what-employees-want-vs-what-their-bosses-think-employees-want#:~:text=This%20survey%20came%20out%20in%201946%20in%20Foreman,%E2%80%9Cin%E2%80%9D%20on%20things%20Sympathetic%20help%20on%20personal%20problems; Grimme, D., and Grimme, S. "Ghr Sample Presentation – Managing the Human Resource." January 20, 2009. Accessed at https://www.slideshare.net/slideshow/ghr-sample-presentation-managing-the-human-resource-presentation/936203; Grimme, D., and Grimme, S. *The New Manager's Tool Kit*. New York: AMACOM, 2008; and Kovach, K. A. "What Motivates Employees? Workers and Supervisors Give Different Answers." *Business Horizons* 30, no. 5 (1987): 58–65.

30. Skilbeck, R. "Rethinking Employee Benefits: 4 Ways to Approach Non-Monetary Rewards." *Forbes*, May 1, 2019. Accessed at https://www.forbes.com/sites/rebeccaskilbeck/2019/04/29/re-thinking-employee-benefits-4-ways-to-approach-non-monetary-rewards/; Silverman, M. "Non-Financial Recognition: The Most Effective of Rewards?" Institute for Employment Studies, 2004. Accessed at https://www.employment-studies.co.uk/system/files/resources/files/mp4.pdf; "The Benefits of Tangible Non-Monetary Incentives." Incentive Research Foundation, 2003. Accessed at https://enterpriseengagement.org/articles/content/8288816/the-benefits-of-tangible-nonmonetary-incentives/; and Graham, G. H. "Going the Extra Mile: Motivating Your Workers Doesn't Always Involve Money." *San Jose Mercury News,* January 7, 1987, p. 4C.

31. Kouzes, J. M., and Posner, B. Z. *The Leadership Challenge: How to Make Extraordinary Things Happen in Organizations* (7th ed.) Hoboken, NJ: Wiley, 2023.

Chapter 2: The Seven Essentials of Encouraging

1. You can watch this scene on "In Search of Excellence: The Video." Video Arts, Inc., and Nathan/Tyler, 1987. Available from Enterprise Media LLC, Cambridge, MA. Accessed July 20, 2024, https://www.enterprisemedia.com/product/00059/in-search-of-excellence-with-tom-peters. To learn more about the Super Person of the Month award, see Melohn, T. *The New Partnership: Profit by Bringing Out the Best in Your People, Customers, and Yourself.* Hoboken, NJ: Wiley, 1994, pp. 127–138.

2. Denning, S. "Telling Tales." *Harvard Business Review*, May–June 2004. Accessed at https://hbr.org/2004/05/telling-tales.

3. Trudel, N., Lockwood, P. L., Rushworth, M. F. S., and Wittmann, M. K. "Neural Activity Tracking Identity and Confidence in Social Information." *eLife* 12:e71315, February 10, 2023. Accessed at https://elifesciences.org/articles/71315; Sealy, R., and Singh, V. "The Importance of Role Models in the Development of Leaders' Professional Identities." A chapter in James, K. T. and Collins, J. (eds.) *Leadership Perspectives: Knowledge into Action.* New York: Palgrave Macmillan, 2008.

4.   For more on the power of social connection, see Robson, D. *The Laws of Connection: The Scientific Secrets of Building a Strong Social Network.* New York: Pegasus Books, 2024.

5.   Kouzes, J. M., and Posner, B. Z. *Credibility: How Leaders Gain and Lose It, Why People Demand It* (2nd ed.). San Francisco: Jossey-Bass, A Wiley Imprint, 2011.

6.   Kouzes, J. M., and Posner, B. Z., *The Leadership Challenge: How to Make Extraordinary Things Happen in Organizations* (7th ed.). Hoboken, NJ: Wiley, 2023.

7.   Kouzes, J. M., and Posner, B. Z. *Leadership Practices Inventory (LPI)* (5th ed.). Hoboken, NJ: Wiley, 2017.

Chapter 3: The Leadership Encouragement Index

1.   Bennis, W. *On Becoming a Leader.* Reading, Mass.: Addison Wesley, 1989, p. 40.

2.   Kouzes, J. M., and Posner, B. Z. *Leadership Practices Inventory (LPI)* (5th ed.) Hoboken, NJ: Wiley, 2017. For information about the LPI, see https://www.leadershipchallenge.com/solutions/lpi360.aspx.

Chapter 4: The First Essential: Set Clear Standards

1.   Carroll, L. *Alice's Adventures in Wonderland and Through the Looking Glass.* New York: Puffin Books, 2015, pp. 101–116. (First published in 1865.)

2.   Cascio, W. F. "Changes in Workers, Work, and Organizations," in *Handbook of Psychology.* Borman, W., Klimoski, R., and Ilgen, D. (eds), vol. 12, chap. 16. Hoboken, NJ: Wiley, 2003. Also see Bailey, C., and Madden, A. "What Makes Work Meaningful—or Meaningless." *MIT Sloan Review,*

June 2016. Accessed at https://sloanreview.mit.edu/article/what-makes-work-meaningful-or-meaningless/#ref2.

3. Lysova, E. I., Fletcher, L., and Baroudi, S. E. "What Makes Work Meaningful?" *Harvard Business Review*, July 12, 2023. Accessed at https://hbr.org/20.23/07/what-makes-work-meaningful.

4. EY Business Institute. "The Business Case for Purpose." 2015. Accessed at https://assets.ey.com/content/dam/ey-sites/ey-com/en_gl/topics/digital/ey-the-business-case-for-purpose.pdf.

5. Ibid.

6. Dhingra, N., Emmett, J., Samo, A., and Schaninger, B. "Igniting Individual Purpose in Times of Crisis." *McKinsey Quarterly*, August 18, 2020. Accessed at https://www.mckinsey.com/capabilities/people-and-organizational-performance/our-insights/igniting-individual-purpose-in-times-of-crisis.

7. Ibid.

8. Cable, D. "Helping Your Team Feel the Purpose in Their Work." *Harvard Business Review*, October 22, 2018. Accessed at https://hbr.org/2019/10/helping-your-team-feel-the-purpose-in-their-work. Also see Gast, A., Illanes, P., Probst, N., Schaninger, B., and Simpson, B. "Purpose: Shifting from Why to How." McKinsey & Company, April 22, 2020. Accessed at https://www.mckinsey.com/capabilities/people-and-organizational-performance/our-insights/purpose-shifting-from-why-to-how.

9. McLeod, L. E., and Lotardo, E. "Don't Let Your Corporate Purpose Get Lost in the Daily Grind." *Harvard Business Review*, November 8, 2023. Accessed at https://hbr.org/2023/11/dont-let-your-corporate-purpose-get-lost-in-the-daily-grind.

10. For example, see Nicita, C. "How Businesses Can Reframe Growth through the Lens of Customer Outcomes." *Forbes*, March 15, 2021. Accessed at https://www.forbes.com/sites/forbesagencycouncil/2021/03/15/how-businesses-can-reframe-growth-through-the-lens-of-customer-outcomes/; and Nash, L., and Stevenson, H. H. "Success That Lasts." *Harvard Business Review* 82, no. 2 (February 2004): 102–109.

11. Eighty-four percent of Girl Scout alums, for example, currently hold leadership positions. Girl Scout Research Institute, "The Girl Scout Alum Difference: A Lifetime of Courage, Confidence, and Character." 2021. Assessed at https://www.girlscouts.org/content/dam/gsusa/

Notes

forms-and-documents/about/research/GSUSA_GSRI_2021_The-Girl-Scout-Alum-Difference_Executive-Summary.pdf.

12. See Posner, B. Z., and Westwood, R. I. "A Cross-Cultural Investigation of the Shared Values Relationship." *International Journal of Value-Based Management* 11, no. 4 (1995): 1–10; Posner, B. Z., and Schmidt, W. H. "Demographic Characteristics and Shared Values." *International Journal of Value-Based Management* 5, no. 1 (1992): 77–87; Posner, B. Z. "Person-Organization Values Congruence: No Support for Individual Differences as a Moderating Influence." *Human Relations* 45, no. 2 (1992): 351–361; Posner, B. Z., Kouzes, J. M., and Schmidt, W. H. "Shared Values Make a Difference: An Empirical Test of Corporate Culture." *Human Resource Management* 24, no. 3 (1985: 293–310. For data on values and health, see, for example, Chapman, J. "Collegial Support Linked to Reduction of Job Stress. *Nursing Management* 24 no. 5 (1993): 52–56; Jex, S. M., and Gudanowski, D. M. "Efficacy Beliefs and Work Stress." *Journal of Organizational Behavior* 13, no. 5 (1992): 509–517; Matteson, M. T. "Individual-Organizational Relationship: Implications for Preventing Job Stress and Burnout." In J. T. Quick and others (eds.), *Work Stress: Health Care Systems in the Workplace*. New York: Praeger, 1987.

13. Posner, B. Z. and Joongoo, H. "How Values and Value Clarity Still Matter: An Extended Study of Global Managers." *Journal of Values-Based Leadership* 17, no. 1 (2024). Accessed at https://scholar.valpo.edu/jvbl/vol17/iss1/7/; Posner, B. Z., and Schmidt, W. H. "Values Congruence and Differences Between the Interplay of Personal and Organizational Value Systems." *Journal of Business Ethics* 12, no. 2 (1992): 171–177.

14. Csikszentmihalyi, M. *Finding Flow: The Psychology of Engagement with Everyday Life*. New York: Basic Books, 1997, p. 137.

15. Ibid., p. 23.

16. Ibid.

17. Bandura, A., and Cervone, D. "Self-Evaluative and Self-Efficacy Mechanisms Governing the Motivational Effects of Goal Systems." *Journal of Personality and Social Psychology,* 1983, vol. 45, pp. 1017–1028.

18. Eden, D., "Leadership and Expectations: Pygmalion Effects and Other Self-Fulfilling Prophecies in Organizations." *Leadership Quarterly* 3, no. 4 (1992): 271–305. http://doi.org/10.1016/1048-9843(92)90018-B; Eden, D. and Ravid, G., "Pygmalion vs. Self-Expectancy: Effects of Instructor and Self-Expectancy

on Trainee Performance." *Organizational Behavior and Human Performance* 30 (1982): 351–364. https://doi.org/10.1016/0030-5073(82)90225-2; Eden, D. and Shani, A. B., "Pygmalion Goes to Boot Camp." *Journal of Applied Psychology* 67 (1982): 194–199. Accessed at https://doi.org/10.1037/0021-9010.67.2.194; Also see Bornstein, J. "How a Lack of Clear Expectations Leaves Employees Anxious and Adrift." *Forbes*, June 5, 2023. Accessed at https://www.forbes.com/sites/forbescoachescouncil/2023/06/05/how-a-lack-of-clear-expectations-leaves-employees-anxious-and-adrift/; Yotsidi, V., Pagoulatou, A., Kyriazos, T., and Stalikas, A. "The Role of Hope in Academic and Work Environments: An Integrative Literature Review." *Psychology* 9 (2018): pp. 385–402; Peterson, S. J., and Byson, K. "Exploring the Role of Hope in Job Performance: Results from Four Studies." *Journal of Organizational Behavior* 29, no. 6 (2008): 785–803.

19.   Porath, C. *Mastering Community: The Surprising Ways Coming Together Moves Us from Surviving to Thriving.* New York: Balance, 2022.

Chapter 5: The Second Essential: Expect the Best

1.   For more on the Pygmalion myth, see https://en.wikipedia.org/wiki/Pygmalion_(mythology).

2.   See Rosenthal, R., and Jacobson, L. *Pygmalion in the Classroom: Teacher Expectation and Pupils' Intellectual Development.* New York: Crown, 2003; and Rosenthal, R., and Jacobson, L. "Pygmalion in the Classroom." *Urban Review* 3, no.1 (1968): 16–20.

3.   See, for example, Niari, M., and Manousou, E. "The Pygmalion Effect in Distance Learning: A Case Study at the Hellenic Open University." *European Journal of Open Distance and E-Learning* 19, no. 1 (2015), doi:10.1515/eurodl-2016-0003; Livingston, J. S. "Pygmalion in Management." *Harvard Business Review,* January–February 2003; Eden, D. "Leadership and Expectations: Pygmalion Effects and Other Self-Fulfilling Prophecies in Organizations." *Leadership Quarterly* 3, no. 4 (1992): 271–305; Yoder, J. D., "Pygmalion in Management: Productivity as a Self-Fulfilling Prophecy." *Academy of Management Review* 16, no. 1 (1991):

Notes

209–212; Eden, D. *Pygmalion in Management: Productivity as a Self-Fulfilling Prophecy.* Lexington, MA: Lexington Books, 1990; Jones, E. C. "Interpreting Interpersonal Behavior: The Effects of Expectancies." *Science* 234 (1986): 41–46; Field, R. H. G., and Van Seters, D. A. "Management by Expectations (MBE): The Power of Positive Prophecy." *Journal of General Management* 14, no. 2 (1988): 1–33.

4.   Manzoni, J.-F., and Barsoux, J.-L. "The Set-Up-to-Fail Syndrome." *Harvard Business Review,* March–April 1998, pp. 101–113; Manzoni, J.-F., and Barsoux, J.-L. *The Set-Up-To-Fail Syndrome: How Good Managers Cause Great People to Fail.* Boston: Harvard Business Review Press, 2002. Also see Gardanova, Z., Nikitina, N., and Strielkowski, W. "Critical Leadership and Set-Up-To-Fail Syndrome." *Advances in Social Science, Education and Humanities Research* 359 (2019), doi:10.2991/icsbal-19.2019.4.

5.   Manzoni and Barsoux, op. cit., p. 102.

6.   "One-Legged Man Scales 14,408-Foot Mt. Rainier." *New York Times,* July 19, 1982, Section A, p. 10. Accessed at https://www.nytimes.com/1982/07/19/us/around-the-nation-one-legged-man-scales-14408-foot-mt-rainier.html.

7.   For a discussion of group effectiveness and positive images, see Cooperrider, D. L. "Positive Image, Positive Action: The Affirmative Basis of Organizing." In Srivastva, S., Cooperrider, D. L., et al., *Appreciative Management and Leadership: The Power of Positive Thought and Action in Organizations.* (San Francisco: Jossey-Bass, 1990), pp. 108, 115. For the original study on group images, see Schwartz, R. "The Internal Dialogue: On the Asymmetry Between Positive and Negative Coping Thoughts." *Cognitive Therapy and Research* 10 (1986): 591–605.

8.   Cooperrider, op. cit., p. 114.

9.   Polak, F. *The Image of the Future.* New York: Elsevier, 1973, p. 19. Quoted in Cooperrider, op. cit., p. 111.

10.   See Spencer, S. J., Logel, C., and Davies, P. G. "Stereotype Threat." *Annual Review of Psychology* 67 (2016): 415–37. Accessed at doi: 10.1146/annurev-psych-073115-103235.

11.   Steele, C. M. "A Threat in the Air: How Stereotypes Shape Intellectual Identity and Performance." *American Psychologist* 52, no. 6 (1997): 613–629. Also see Eberhardt, J. L. *Biased: Uncovering the Hidden Prejudice That Shapes What We See, Think, and Do.* New York: Penguin, 2020; Johnson, W. B., and Smith, D. G. "Mentoring Someone with Imposter Syndrome." *Harvard*

Business Review, February 22, 2019. Accessed at https://hbr.org/2019/
02/mentoring-someone-with-imposter-syndrome; and Steele, C. M. *Whis-
tling Vivaldi: How Stereotypes Affect Us and What We Can Do*. New York: W.
W. Norton, 2011.

12. Gomez-Jorge, F., and Diaz-Garrido, E. "The Relation Between Self-Esteem
and Productivity: An Analysis in Higher Education Institutions." *Frontiers
in Psychology* 13 (2023), https://doi.org/10.3389%2Ffpsyg.2022.1112437;
Orth, U., and Robins, R. W. "Is High Self-Esteem Beneficial? Revising a
Classic Question." *American Psychologist* 77, no. 1 (2022): 5–17; Leary, M.
R. "The Social and Psychological Importance of Self-Esteem." In Kowalski,
R. M., and Leary, M. R. (eds.). *The Social Psychology of Emotional and
Behavioral Problems: Interfaces of Social and Clinical Psychology*. Wash,
DC: American Psychological Association, 1999, pp. 197–221; Blitzer, R.
J., Petersen, C., and Rogers, L. "How to Build Self-Esteem." *Training and
Development* 47 (1993): 58–60.

13. Wood, R., and Bandura, A. "Impact of Conceptions of Ability on Self-
Regulatory Mechanisms and Complex Decision Making." *Journal of
Personality and Social Psychology* 56, no. 3 (1989): 407–415. This research
foreshadowed the work of Carol Dweck on growth and fixed mindset. For
an in-depth discussion of these constructs and their effects, see Dweck,
C. S. *Mindset: The New Psychology of Success*. New York: Ballantine Books,
2016. Also see Kouzes. T. K. and Posner, B. Z. "Influence of Managers'
Mindset on Leadership Behavior." *Leadership and Organization Development Journal* 40, no. 8 (2019): 829–844. Accessed at https://doi
.org/10.1108/LODJ-03-2019-0142.

Chapter 6: The Third Essential: Pay Attention

1. For an in-depth discussion of personal credibility, see Kouzes, J. M.,
and Posner, B. Z. *Credibility: How Leaders Gain and Lose It, Why People
Demand It* (2nd ed). San Francisco: Jossey-Bass, 2011.

2. Fisher, R., and Brown, S. *Getting Together*. Boston: Houghton
Mifflin, 1988.

3. McCall, M. W., Lombardo, M., and Morrison, A. *The Lessons of Experience.* Lexington, MA: Lexington Books, 1988.

5. Srivastva, S., and Barrett, F. J. "Foundations for Executive Integrity: Dialogue, Diversity, Development." In Srivastva, S., and Associates (eds.), *Executive Integrity.* San Francisco: Jossey-Bass, 1988.

6. As quoted in "The Value of Listening: Annette Bening," California Shakespeare Theater, March 6, 2024. Accessed at https://calshakes.org/the-value-of-listening-annette-bening/.

7. As cited in Rice, F., "Champions of Communications." *Fortune*, June 3, 1991, pp. 111ff.

8. O'Donnell, R. "Employee Listening: Why Embracing Workplace Feedback Matters." October 2020. Accessed at https://www.trinet.com/insights/listening-to-employees-its-more-important-than-you-think.

9. The Workforce Institute. "The Heard and the Heard-Nots." UKG, June 22, 2021. Accessed at https://www.ukg.com/blog/workforce-institute/new-research-the-heard-and-the-heard-nots.

10. Jehn, K. A., and Shah, P. P. "Interpersonal Relationships and Task Performance: An Examination of Mediating Processes in Friendship and Acquaintance Groups." *Journal of Personality and Social Psychology* 72, no. 4 (1997): 775–790. Also see Chung, S., Lount, R. B., Park, H. M., Park, E. S "Friends With Performance Benefits: A Meta-Analysis on the Relationship Between Friendship and Group Performance." *Personality and Social Psychology Bulletin* 44, no. 1 (2017): 63–79; and Ross, J. A. "Does Friendship Improve Job Performance?" *Harvard Business Review,* March–April 1997.

11. Patel, A., and Plowman, S. "The Increasing Importance of a Best Friend at Work." Gallup, January 19, 2024. Accessed at https://www.gallup.com/workplace/397058/increasing-importance-best-friend-work.aspx. Also see Clifton, J. "The Power of Work Friends." *Harvard Business Review,* October 7, 2022. Accessed at https://hbr.org/2022/10/the-power-of-work-friends.

12. Offermann, L., and Rosh, L. "Building Trust Through Self-Disclosure." *Harvard Business Review*, June 13, 2012. Accessed at https://hbr.org/2012/06/instantaneous-intimacy-skillfu; Sprecher, S., Treger, S., Wondra, J. D., Hilaire, N., and Wallpe, K. Taking Turns: Reciprocal Self-Disclosure Promotes Liking in Initial Interactions. *Journal of Experimental Social Psychology* 49, no. 5 (2013): 860–866; Laurenceau, J. P., Barrett, L.

F., and Pietromonaco, P. R. "Intimacy as an Interpersonal Process: The Importance of Self-Disclosure, Partner Disclosure, and Perceived Partner Responsiveness in Interpersonal Exchanges." *Journal of Personality and Social Psychology* 74, no. 5 (1998): 1238–1251.

13. Sherf, E. N., Gajendran, R. F., and Posner, B. Z. "Seeking and Finding Justice: Why and When Managers' Feedback Seeking Enhances Justice Enactment." *Journal of Organizational Behavior* 42, no. 6 (2021): 741–766; Porter, J. "6 Steps Leaders Can Take to Get the Most Out of Feedback." *Harvard Business Review*, September 10, 2019. Accessed at https://hbr .org/2019/09/6-steps-leaders-can-take-to-get-the-most-out-of-feedback; Stone, D., Heen, S. *Thanks for the Feedback: The Science and Art of Receiving Feedback Well.* New York: Penguin Books, 2015; Kouzes, J. M., and Posner, B. Z. "To Get Honest Feedback, Leaders Need to Ask." *Harvard Business Review*, February 27, 2014. Accessed at https://hbr.org/2014/02/ to-get-honest-feedback-leaders-need-to-ask.

Chapter 7: The Fourth Essential: Personalize Recognition

1. For more on this, see Gibson, K. R., O'Leary, K., and Weintraub, J. R. "The Little Things That Make Employees Feel Appreciated." *Harvard Business Review*, January 23, 2020. Accessed at https://hbr.org/2020/01/the-little-things-that-make-employees-feel-appreciated.

2. Johnson, W., and Humble, A. "Notes of Appreciation Can Boost Individual and Team Morale." *Harvard Business Review*, November 21, 2022. Accessed at https://hbr.org/2022/11/notes-of-appreciation-can-boost-individual-and-team-morale.

3. O'Flaherty, S., Sanders, M. T., and Whillans, A. "Research: A Little Recognition Can Provide a Big Morale Boost." *Harvard Business Review*, March 29, 2021. Accessed at https://hbr.org/2021/03/research-a-little-recognition-can-provide-a-big-morale-boost.

4. Gostick, A., and Elton, C. *Leading with Gratitude: Eight Business Practices for Extraordinary Business Results.* New York: HarperCollins, 2020.

5. Jones, B. "How Positive Reinforcement Keeps Employees Engaged."
    Harvard Business Review, February 28, 2017. Accessed at https://hbr.org/
    sponsored/2017/02/how-positive-reinforcement-keeps-employees-engaged.

6. Kube, S., Maréchal, M. A., and Puppe, C. "The Currency of Reciprocity:
    Gift Exchange in the Workplace." *American Economic Review* 102 no. 4
    (2012): 1644–1662.

Chapter 8: The Fifth Essential: Tell the Story

1. King, S. "Carrie: The Bestseller I Threw in the Bin." *Guardian*. September
    17, 2000. Accessed at https://www.theguardian.com/books/2000/sep/17/
    stephenking.fiction.

2. Martin, J., and Powers, M. "Organizational Stories: More Vivid and
    Persuasive Than Quantitative Data." In B. M. Staw (ed.), *Psychological
    Foundations of Organizational Behavior* (2nd ed.) Glenview, IL: Scott,
    Foresman, 1983; see pp. 161–168. Also see Cecchi-Dimeglio, P. "Why
    Sharing Good News Matters" *MIT Sloan Management Review*, June 17,
    2020. Accessed at https://sloanreview.mit.edu/article/why-sharing-good-
    news-matters/; Pink, D. *To Sell Is Human: The Surprising Truth About
    Moving Others*. New York: Penguin Group, 2012; Hsu, J. "The Secrets of
    Storytelling: Why We Love a Good Yarn." *Scientific American*, August 1,
    2008. Accessed at https://www.scientificamerican.com/article/the-secrets-
    of-storytelling/.

3. Spence, G. *How to Win an Argument Every Time*. New York: St. Martin's
    Press, 1995, p. 113.

4. Wilkens, A. L. "Organizational Stories as Symbols Which Control the
    Organization." In L. R. Pondy and others (eds.), *Organizational Symbol-
    ism*. Greenwich, CT: JAI Press, 1983. Also see Heath, C., and Heath,
    D. Made to Stick: Why Some Ideas Survive, *and Others Die*. New York:
    Random House, 2007; Conger, J. A. *Winning 'Em Over: A New Model for
    Management in the Age of Persuasion*. New York: Simon & Schuster, 1998;
    Armstrong, D. *Managing by Storying Around: A New Method of Leader-
    ship*. New York: Doubleday Currency, 1992.

Notes

5. Shaw, G., Brown, R., and Bromiley, P. "Strategic Stories: How 3M Is Rewriting Business Planning." *Harvard Business Review*, May–June 1998, pp. 41–50.

6. Weick, K. E. *Sensemaking in Organizations*. Thousand Oaks, CA: Sage Publications, 1995, pp. 60–61.

7. Klein, G. *The Sources of Power: How People Make Decisions*. Cambridge, MA: MIT Press, 1998.

8. Bonchek, M. "How to Build a Strategic Narrative." *Harvard Business Review*, March 25, 2016. Accessed at https://hbr.org/2016/03/how-to-build-a-strategic-narrative.

9. Barney, J. B., Amorim, M., and Júlio, C. *The Secret of Culture Change: How to Build Authentic Stories That Transform Your Organization*. Oakland, CA: Berrett-Koehler, 2023.

10. Yoon, J., Blunden, H., Kristal, A., and Whillans, A. "Why Asking for Advice Is More Effective Than Asking for Feedback." *Harvard Business Review*, September 20, 2019. Accessed at https://hbr.org/2019/09/why-asking-for-advice-is-more-effective-than-asking-for-feedback; Liljenquist, and Galinsky, A. D. "Win Over an Opponent by Asking for Advice." *Harvard Business Review*, June 27, 2014. Accessed at https://hbr.org/2014/06/win-over-an-opponent-by-asking-for-advice.

11. Fitzgerald, K., Paravati, E., Green, M. C., Moore, M., and Qian, J. (2020). "Restorative Narratives for Health Promotion." *Health Communication* 35, no. 3 (2020): 356–363. Accessed at https://pubmed.ncbi.nlm.nih.gov/30614737/.

12. Zak, P. J. "How Stories Change the Brain." *Greater Good Magazine*, December 17, 2013. Accessed at https://greatergood.berkeley.edu/article/item/how_stories_change_brain.

13. Westergaard, N. "5 Types of Stories Leaders Need to Tell." *Harvard Business Review*, September 22, 2023. Accessed at https://hbr.org/2023/09/5-types-of-stories-leaders-need-to-tell.

14. Gardner, H. *Leading Minds*. New York: Basic Books, 1995, p. 43.

15. Tichy, N., with Cohen, E. *The Leadership Engine: How Winning Companies Build Leaders at Every Level*. New York: HarperBusiness, 1997, p. 173.

16. Frei, F. X., and Morriss, A. "Storytelling That Drives Bold Change." *Harvard Business Review*, November–December 2023. Accessed at https://hbr.org/2023/11/storytelling-that-drives-bold-change

17. As mentioned in this video clip: https://www.oprah.com/own-essenceblackwomeninhollywood/the-aha-moment-that-changed-ava-duvernays-life.

18. Klein, op. cit., pp. 177–178.

19. For more on becoming a great storyteller, see Frei, F. X., and Morriss, A. *Move Fast and Fix Things: The Trusted Leader's Guide to Solving Hard Problems*. Boston: Harvard Business Review Press, 2023; and Moth, The, Bowles, M., Burns, C., Hixton, J., Jenness, S. A., and Tellers, K. *How to Tell a Story: The Essential Guide to Memorable Storytelling from The Moth*. New York: Crown, 2023.

20. McCarthy, J. F. "Short Stories at Work." *Group & Organization Management* 33, no. 2 (2008): 163–193.

21. Clark, C. "How Family Stories Help Children Weather Hard Times." Emery News Center, April 29, 2020. Accessed at https://news.emory.edu/stories/2020/04/esc_covid_19_family_stories/campus.html.

22. These statistics are from Statistica, an online global data and business intelligence platform. Accessed July 25, 2024, at https://www.statista.com/statistics/1253972/zoom-daily-meeting-participants-global/#:~:text=By%20April%202020%2C%20Zoom%20Video,at%2010%20million%20meeting%20participants.

Chapter 9: The Sixth Essential: Celebrate Together

1. Jones, M. O., and et al. "Performing Well: The Impact of Rituals, Celebrations, and Networks of Support." Presented at the Western Academy of Management conference, Hollywood, California, April 10, 1987. Also see Kim, T., Sezer, O., Schroeder, J., Risen, J., Gino, F., and Norton, M. L. "Work Group Rituals Enhance the Meaning of Work." *Organizational Behavior and Human Decision Processes* 165 (2021): 197–212; and Howard, S. G. "How to Unlock the Creative Magic at Your Company." *Inc.*, May 13, 2016. Accessed at https://www.inc.com/suzanne-gibbs-howard/5-steps-rituals-creative-culture.html.

Notes

2. Deal, T., and Key, M. K. *Corporate Celebration: Play, Purpose, and Profit at Work.* San Francisco: Berrett-Koehler, 1998, p. 11.

3. For example, see Sheridan, R. *Chief Joy Officer: How Great Leaders Elevate Human Energy and Eliminate Fear.* New York: Penguin Random House, 2018; Yerkes, L. *Fun Works: Creating Places Where People Love to Work.* Oakland, CA: Berrett-Koehler, 2001; Hemsath, D., and Yerkes, L. *301 Ways to Have Fun at Work.* San Francisco: Berrett-Koehler, 1997; Basso, B., and Klosek, J. *This Job Should Be Fun! The New Profit Strategy for Managing People in Tough Times.* Holbrook, MA: Bob Adams, Inc., 1991.

4. McDowell, T., Ehteshami, S., and Sandell, K. "Are You Having Fun Yet?' *Deloitte Review* 24 (January 2019): 136. Accessed at https://www2.deloitte .com/content/dam/insights/us/articles/4803_DR24_Are-you-having-fun-yet/DI_DR24_Are-you-having-fun-yet.pdf.

5. Ornish, D. *Love and Survival: The Scientific Basis for the Healing Power of Love and Intimacy.* New York: HarperCollins, 1998. See especially pp. 23–71 for a review of several significant studies on the relationship between social relationships and health.

6. Ibid., p. 23.

7. Ibid., p. 28.

8. See Donovan, N. J., and Blazer, D. "Social Isolation and Loneliness in Older Adults: Review and Commentary of a National Academies Report." *American Journal of Geriatric Psychiatry* 28, no. 12 (2020): 1233–1244. Accessed at https://www.ncbi.nlm.nih.gov/pmc/articles/PMC7437541/; and World Health Organization, "Social Isolation and Loneliness." Accessed at https://www.who.int/teams/social-determinants-of-health/ demographic-change-and-healthy-ageing/social-isolation-and-loneliness#:~:text=Social%20isolation%20and%20loneliness%20are%20 widespread%2C%20with%20an%20estimated%201,cent%20of%20 adolescents%20experiencing%20loneliness.

9. Ornish, op. cit., p. 30.

10. Pinker, S. *The Village Effect: How Face-to-Face Contact Can Make Us Healthier and Happier.* Vintage Canada, 2015.

11. Friedman, R. "5 Things High-Performing Teams Do Differently." *Harvard Business* Review, October 21, 2021. Accessed at https://hbr.org/2021/10/5-things-high-performing-teams-do-differently.

12. Waldinger, R. and Schulz, M., *The Good Life: Lessons from the World's Longest Scientific Study of Happiness.* New York: Simon & Schuster, 2023, p. 10.

13. Ibid., p. 29.

14. Grant, A. M., and Gino, F. "A Little Thanks Goes a Long Way: Explaining Why Gratitude Expressions Motivate Prosocial Behavior." *Journal of Personality and Social Psychology* 98, no. 6 (2010): 946–955.

15. See Fossilen, L. and West-Duffy, M. "How to Create Belonging for Remote Workers." *MIT Sloan Management Review*, February 8, 2019. Accessed at https://sloanreview.mit.edu/article/how-to-create-belonging-for-remote-workers/; Hill, N. S., and Bartol, K. M. "Five Ways to Improve Communication in Virtual Teams." *MIT Sloan Management Review*, June 13, 2018. Accessed at https://sloanreview.mit.edu/article/five-ways-to-improve-communication-in-virtual-teams/.

16. Deal, T. E., and Key, M. A. *Corporate Celebration: Play, Purpose, and Profit at Work*. New York: Penguin Random House, 1998.

17. O'Flaherty, S., Sanders, M. T., and Whillans, A. "Research: A Little Recognition Can Provide a Big Morale Boost." *Harvard Business Review*, March 29, 2021. Accessed at https://hbr.org/2021/03/research-a-little-recognition-can-provide-a-big-morale-boost.

18. Bradler, C., Dur, R., Neckermann, S., and Non, A. "Employee Recognition and Performance: A Field Experiment." *Management Science* 62, no. 11 (2016): 3085–3391.

19. Campbell, D. "If I'm in Charge Here, Why Is Everybody Laughing?" Greensboro, NC: Center for Creative Leadership, 1984, p. 64.

20. DeForest, C. "The Art of Celebration: A New Concept for Today's Leaders." In J. D. Adams (ed.), *Transforming Leadership: From Vision to Results*. Alexandria, VA: Miles River Press, 1986, p. 223.

21. Nelson, B. *1001 Ways to Reward Employees*. New York: Workman Publishing, 1994.

Chapter 10: The Seventh Essential: Set the Example

1. Conant, D. *TouchPoints: Creating Powerful Leadership Connections in the Smallest of Moments*. San Francisco: Jossey-Bass, 2011.

Notes

2. As reported in Frei, F. X., and Morriss, A. "Storytelling That Drives Bold Change." *Harvard Business Review*, November–December 2023.

3. McDowell, T., Ehteshami, S., and Sandell, K. "Are You Having Fun Yet? *Deloitte Review* 24 (January 2019). Accessed at https://www2.deloitte.com/ content/dam/insights/us/articles/4803_DR24_Are-you-having-fun-yet/ DI_DR24_Are-you-having-fun-yet.pdf.

4. Fehr, R., Fulmer, A., Awtrey, E., Miller, J. A., "The Grateful Workplace: A Multilevel Model of Gratitude in Organizations." *Academy of Management Review* 42, no. 2 (2016). https://doi.org/10.5465/amr.2014.0374.

5. For details on our research on leader credibility, see Kouzes, J. M., and Posner, B. Z. *Credibility: How Leaders Gain and Lose It, Why People Demand It* (2nd ed.). San Francisco: Jossey-Bass, 2011; Kouzes, J. M., and Posner, B. Z. *The Truth About Leadership: The No-Fads, Heart-of-the-Matter Facts You Need to Know*. San Francisco, Jossey-Bass, 2010.

6. Kouzes, J. M., and Posner, B. Z., *The Leadership Challenge: How to Make Extraordinary Things Happen in Organizations* (7th ed.). Hoboken, NJ: Wiley, 2023. This is the premise of our forthcoming book, *The Radical Promise: Doing What You Say You Will Do*.

7. Ibid., p. 25.

8. Lamott, A. *Bird by Bird: Some Instructions on Writing and Life*. New York: Pantheon, 1994, p. 19.

9. Nelson, B. *1,000 Ways to Engage Employees*. Newburyport, MA: Career Press, 2018; *1,001 Ways to Energize Employees*. New York: Workman Publishing, 1997; *1,001 Ways to Reward Employees*. New York: Workman Publishing, 1994.

10. Goulston, M. "What to Do When Praise Makes You Uncomfortable." *Harvard Business Review*, December 13, 2013. Accessed at https://hbr .org/2013/12/what-to-do-when-praise-makes-you-uncomfortable.

11. Littlefield, C. "How to Write a Meaningful Thank You Note." *Harvard Business Review*, November 12, 2021. Accessed at https://hbr.org/2021/11/ how-to-write-a-meaningful-thank-you-note; and Littlefield, C. "How to Give and Receive Compliments at Work." *Harvard Business Review*, October 12, 2019. Accessed at https://hbr.org/2019/10/how-to-give-and-receive-compliments-at-work.

Chapter 11: Leadership Is an Affair of the Heart

1. Palmer, P. J., *Let Your Life Speak: Listening for the Voice of Vocation.* San Francisco: Jossey-Bass, 2000, p. 76.

2. Burnison, G. *Love, Hope and Leadership: A Special Edition.* Hoboken, NJ: Wiley, 2024, p. 255.

3. Porath, C. L., Gerbasi, A., and Schorch, S. L. "The Effects of Civility on Advice, Leadership, and Performance." *Journal of Applied Psychology* 100, no. 5 (2015): 1527–1541. Also see Porath, C. L., and Gerbasi, A. "Does Civility Pay?" *Organizational Dynamics* 44, no. 4 (2015): 281–286; and Porath, C. L., *Mastering Civility: A Manifesto for the Workplace.* New York: Balance, 2016.

4. Kitterman, T. "How Caring Leaders Create High Performance Workplaces." *Great Place to Work Insights,* June 24, 2024. Accessed at https://www.greatplacetowork.com/resources/blog/how-caring-leaders-create-high-performance-workplaces.

5. Willett, J. F., LaGree, D., Shin, H., Houston, J. B., and Duffy, M. "The Role of Leader Communication in Fostering Respectful Workplace Culture and Increasing Employee Engagement and Well-Being." *International Journal of Business Communication* 1–25 (August 2023): 15. Accessed at doi: 10.1177/23294884231195614.

6. For details and data about learning to lead, see Kouzes, J. M., and Posner, B. Z. *Learning Leadership: The Five Fundamentals of Becoming an Exemplary Leader.* San Francisco: The Leadership Challenge, A Wiley Brand, 2016.

ACKNOWLEDGMENTS

WHEN WRITING A book, two things are foremost in our minds—the story and the people. And you can't have one without the other. The story is the people. Not one word of this new edition of *Encouraging the Heart* would have made it to print without the loving support of others. That's the central message of this book: Encouragement from others inspires us to put forth our best efforts and gives them meaning and purpose.

Our spouses are the first and last to share both our joy and struggles. Tae Kouzes and Jackie Schmidt Posner are always there for us. They're our inspiration, our cheering section, and our collective shoulders to lean on. When it comes to encouraging the heart, they exemplify what it's all about. We love you very much.

New editions of any book are always a challenge; they require keeping the best of the past, honoring the current realities, and anticipating what will be relevant in the future. We are grateful to our colleagues at John Wiley & Sons for supporting us in making this happen. Our Associate Publisher, Jeanenne Ray, was immediately on board when we proposed this project. Michelle Hacker, Senior Managing Editor, along with Editorial Assistant Sherri-Anne Forde, kept us on task and on time,

Acknowledgments

especially when the pressure of deadlines approached. Copy editor Amy Handy brought needed clarity and coherence to our writing, and Suganya Selvaraj, Content Refinement Specialist, added expertise to those efforts. No book would have made it into the hands of readers without the dedicated efforts of the marketing team led by Michael Friedberg, Director of Marketing.

New editions of books wouldn't be possible if it weren't for the work of those who were part of the first edition, and we want to again say thanks to a few folks who were part of that process. Kathy Dalle-Molle, Mary Garrett, and Judith Hibbard were among those who contributed editorially. Our EMBA students at the Leavey School of Business, Santa Clara University, along with Ron Crossland, Jeni Nichols, Dick Heller, Christy Tonge, and Steve Farber, contributed stories, suggested candidates for stories, and gave us notes on how we could improve the early drafts.

Hundreds of others have shaped our thinking about leadership and about encouraging the heart. We thank all of those clients, colleagues, students, and friends who have been with us on past leadership expeditions and all those who continue to share our ongoing leadership adventures. Your stories have inspired us and reminded us about the nobility of the human spirit, our capacity for empathy, and the power of love in professional and personal relationships.

We thank all of you for encouraging our hearts over these past four decades as we've studied, practiced, taught, listened, read, observed, written, and marveled at the art of leadership.

James M. Kouzes
Orinda, California

Barry Z. Posner
Berkeley, California

ABOUT THE AUTHORS

JIM KOUZES AND BARRY POSNER have been working together for more than forty years, studying leaders, researching leadership, conducting leadership development seminars, and providing leadership in various capacities, with and without titles. They are coauthors of the award-winning, best-selling book *The Leadership Challenge*, which has sold more than three million copies worldwide and is available in more than twenty-two languages. It has won numerous awards, including the Critics' Choice Award from the nation's book review editors and book-of-the-year awards from the American Council of Healthcare Executives and Fast Company. *The Leadership Challenge* is listed in *The Top 100 Business Books of All Time* as one of the Top 10 books on leadership.

The Student Leadership Challenge: Five Practices for Becoming an Exemplary Leader (now in its fourth edition) has become a standard leadership development book and resource for young people and students from middle to high school, undergraduate to graduate levels. More than five hundred colleges and universities use this book and The Student Leadership Practices Inventory in their classes, seminars, programs, and workshops.

Jim and Barry have co-authored more than a dozen other award-winning leadership books, including *Everyday People, Extraordinary Leadership; Leadership in Higher Education; Stop Selling & Start Leading; Learning Leadership: The Five Fundamentals for Becoming an Exemplary Leader; Turning Adversity into Opportunity; Finding the Courage to Lead; Great Leadership Creates Great Workplaces; Credibility: How Leaders Gain and Lose It, Why People Demand It; The Truth About Leadership: The No-Fads, Heart-of-the-Matter Facts You Need to Know; Encouraging the Heart: A Leader's Guide to Recognizing and Rewarding Others; A Leader's Legacy; Extraordinary Leadership in Australia and New Zealand;* and *Making Extraordinary Things Happen in Asia.*

Jim and Barry developed the widely used and highly acclaimed Leadership Practices Inventory (LPI) and The Student Leadership Practices Inventory (S-LPI). These 360-degree questionnaires provide insights into how frequently leaders use empirically identified behaviors as essential to bringing out the best in people and teams. Worldwide, nearly one million students have completed the S-LPI, and more than five million people have taken the LPI.

Over a thousand research studies have been based on The Five Practices of Exemplary Leadership® framework. More information about these books, inventories, and studies is available at www.leadershipchallenge.com.

Among the honors and awards that Jim and Barry have received are the Association for Talent and Development's (ATD) highest award for their Distinguished Contribution to Workplace Learning and Performance, named Management/Leadership Educators of the Year by the International Management Council, ranked by *Leadership Excellence* magazine in the top 20 on their list of the Top 100 Thought Leaders; named by Coaching for Leadership in the Top 50 Leadership Coaches in the nation; considered by *HR* magazine as one of the Most Influential International Thinkers; and listed among the Top 75 Management Experts in the World by *Inc.* magazine.

Jim and Barry are frequent keynote speakers, and each has conducted leadership development programs for hundreds of organizations, including

Apple, Applied Materials, ARCO, AT&T, Australia Institute of Management, Australia Post, Bank of America, Bose, Charles Schwab, Cisco Systems, Clorox, Community Leadership Association, Conference Board of Canada, Consumers Energy, Deloitte Touche, Department of Energy, Dow Chemical, Egon Zehnder International, Federal Express, Genentech, Google, Gymboree, Hewlett-Packard, IBM, Jobs DR-Singapore, Johnson & Johnson, Kaiser Foundation Health Plans and Hospitals, Intel, Itaú Unibanco, L.L. Bean, Lawrence Livermore National Labs, Lucile Packard Children's Hospital, Mayo Clinic, Merck, Motorola, NetApp, Northrop Grumman, Novartis, Oakwood Housing, Oracle, Petronas, Roche Bioscience, Siemens, 3M, Topgolf/Callaway Brands, Toyota, U.S. Postal Service, United Way, USAA, Verizon, VISA, Westpac, and the Walt Disney Company. In addition, they have presented seminars and lectures at more than 100 college and university campuses.

JIM KOUZES is a Doerr Institute for New Leaders at Rice University fellow and has been the Dean's Executive Fellow of Leadership at the Leavey School of Business, Santa Clara University. He lectures on leadership worldwide to corporations, governments, and nonprofits. He is a highly regarded leadership scholar and an experienced executive. The *Wall Street Journal* hailed him as one of the twelve best executive educators in the United States. Jim has received the Thought Leadership Award from the Instructional Systems Association, the most prestigious award from the trade association of training and development industry providers, and the Golden Gavel, the highest honor awarded by Toastmasters International.

Jim served as president, CEO, and chairman of the Tom Peters Company for eleven years and led the Executive Development Center at Santa Clara University for seven years. He was the founder and executive director of the Joint Center for Human Services Development at San Jose State University for eight years and previously on the School of Social Work, University of Texas staff. His career in training and development began in 1969 when he conducted seminars for Community Action Agency staff and volunteers in the war on poverty. Following graduation from Michigan State University (BA with honors in political science), he served as a

Peace Corps volunteer (1967–1969). You can reach Jim directly at jim@ kouzes.com.

BARRY POSNER chairs the Management and Entrepreneurship Department at the Leavey School of Business, Santa Clara University, where he previously served for six years as associate dean for graduate education, six years as associate dean for executive education, and twelve years as Dean of the School. He holds the Michael J. Accolti, S.J. Professorship, and teaches undergraduate and graduate course in leadership. He has been a distinguished visiting professor around the globe, including Hong Kong University of Science and Technology, Sabanci University (Istanbul), University of Western Australia, University of Auckland (New Zealand), and Seattle University.

At Santa Clara, Barry has received the President's Distinguished Faculty Award, the Leavey School's Extraordinary Faculty Award, and several other outstanding teaching and academic honors. An internationally renowned scholar and educator, he is the author or co-author of more than 100 research and practitioner-focused articles. He serves on the editorial review board for the *Leadership and Organizational Development Journal, Journal of Business Ethics, Administrative Sciences*, and *Frontiers in Psychology*.

Barry received his baccalaureate degree with honors in political science from the University of California, Santa Barbara; his master's degree in public administration from The Ohio State University; and his doctoral degree in organizational behavior and administrative theory from the University of Massachusetts, Amherst. He has consulted worldwide with many public and private sector organizations and works strategically with several community-based and professional organizations. Barry is currently on the board of the Berkeley Food Network and has served previously on the board of the American Institute of Architects (AIA), Big Brothers/Big Sisters of Santa Clara County, Center for Excellence in Nonprofits, Junior Achievement of Silicon Valley and Monterey Bay, Public Allies, San Jose Repertory Theater, SVCreates, Sigma Phi Epsilon Fraternity, Uplift Family Services, and several startup companies. Barry can be reached at bposner@scu.edu.

INDEX

Index

Index